DOWN-TO-EARTH
ASTROLOGY

A REALISTIC APPROACH TO YOUR STARS

DOWN-TO-EARTH
ASTROLOGY

STEPHANIE MICHAELS

ANGUS
& ROBERTSON
PUBLISHERS

ANGUS & ROBERTSON PUBLISHERS

*Unit 4, Eden Park, 31 Waterloo Road,
North Ryde, NSW, Australia 2113, and
16 Golden Square, London W1R 4BN,
United Kingdom*

*First published in Australia
by Angus & Robertson Publishers in 1988
First published in the United Kingdom
by Angus & Robertson (UK) in 1988*

Copyright © Stephanie Michaels 1988

*National Library of Australia
Cataloguing-in-publication data.*

*Michaels, Stephanie, 1945– .
  Down-to-earth astrology.*

  *Bibliography.
  ISBN 0 207 15726 X.*

  1. Astrology. I. Title.

133.5

**Typeset in 12pt Bem by Setrite Typesetters
Printed in Australia by The Book Printer**

CONTENTS

PART III FUNCTION

INTRODUCTION

As a practising astrologer for some eight years, I was constantly confronted with — and astounded by — the superstitious and suspicious attitudes that still prevail towards astrology. This has been the prime motivation for writing this book, which is an effort to banish the 'fortune-telling' aura that still surrounds this subject.

My attitude may seem surprising given that my great-great-grandmother was a Romany gypsy. Romantic as such ancestry may seem, unfortunately by the time I came into the picture all that remained of this colourful heritage were a few dark-eyed relatives and a a lot of superstition. Sadly, I had not inherited any gypsy magic. I became a secretary, which was nevertheless to become significant in the development of this book.

In 1973, however, my heritage caught up with me in a way for, during a period of crisis that left me wandering around the world wondering what life was all about, a friend gave me an astrology book. In that book I found some crucial answers: answers that created a lot more questions and led eventually to the accumulation of an extensive library on astrology and related subjects. During the course of this growing interest, I spent several years as a temporary secretary, which meant moving about from office to office, meeting a lot more people than I otherwise would have. Frequently, as soon as my astrology interests were discovered, I was inundated with questions about my workmates' futures: questions often asked with a bit too much trust for my comfort. This too finally provoked me to attempt here to clear away some of the misunderstandings about the omnipotence of the subject and of its proponents. The more I read, the more I realised that there were many discrepancies and much disagreement among astrologers. So much so that, except for the basic principles established thousands of years ago, it became apparent that it was not safe to trust in the so-called facts that were being stated so confidently by many astrologers.

So this book is also aimed at shaking up a few convictions and questioning certain claims, such as that astrology is a science. It also aims to expose certain misrepresentations which some astrologers foster in the minds of the public.

Too many people trustingly pick their astrologers at random from advertisements in astrology journals, magazines and other publications. They send off their money, and their fates, with little care — as if, by the act of advertising, the person behind the name is automatically capable and honest. Or they choose an astrologer because he or she is a public figure — under the misapprehension that because he or she is 'famous', then he or she is naturally also reputable. It is surprising how many people seem to have blind faith in the honesty and integrity of astrologers, despite the warnings we have had over the last few thousand years. So for those who intend to consult an astrologer this book contains some strong advice.

As many laypeople do not realise the full extent and range of what astrology has to offer, I have listed and examined many of the issues on which an astrologer can be specifically consulted.

I have also tried to show astrology's limitations — especially in the field of prediction, which is the best-known aspect of astrology, as well as the most misused.

PART I

FORM

1 FORTUNE-TELLER

When I was seven years old, I cut out a 'Wheel of Fortune' from a women's magazine and took it to school. It was an instant hit. My peers then were as eager as my peers are today, thirty-five years later, for me to read their fates and fortunes — and with the same unchallenged authority. It did not in the least concern the seven-year-olds to be told that they were destined to meet 'tall, dark strangers', 'go on long journeys to foreign lands', or 'be successful (or fail) in business ventures'. It did not concern them because the fortune was not as important as the mystery associated with fortune-telling. To us, such matters were automatically associated with gypsies, who often camped in the local woods and fields and who were unpredictable, enigmatic and commonly viewed with suspicion by the rest of the population. When gypsy women, selling their pegs, knocked on our doors, our mothers bought them whether they needed them or not. I suspect that the tradition of crossing a gypsy woman's palm with silver persisted more as an insurance against a curse, which was sometimes the outcome of refusing the gypsy's wares, than as payment for a hint about the future — and a few pegs thrown in.

Gypsy curses may not be as common these days but many superstitious omens still exist: walking under ladders; black cats; special lucky and unlucky numbers and colours — not to mention old wives' tales and fairy stories about witches and magic. As children we revel in all this, we soak it up. And it becomes a part of the subconscious and percolates into our adult life, affecting our choices and actions more than we would care to imagine.

In fact, contrary to what our mushrooming intellectual and scientific enlightenment suggests, superstition is alive and well and growing in power as a result of the rational mind's efforts to suppress the irrational. No matter how deeply science penetrates Nature's mysteries, no matter how much we dissect, label and categorise our universe for our intellectual security, the fundamental questions about 'life, the universe, and everything' remain unanswered. Consequently, we are still held captive by our instinctive and primitive fear of the unknown.

Here we are, about to enter the twenty-first century, landing men on the Moon, sending probes hurtling off to the outer limits of our solar system — and yet printing adult magazines that cater to, and encourage, these 'silly superstitions'. No matter how down-to-earth or scientific astrologers try to be in their self-presentation, we are as superstitious of them now as we were of gypsies and their ilk in less sophisticated times . . . because astrology has come to us straight out of the depths of a mythical past when astrology and magic were one. The astrologer is a caricature: the gypsy hovering over her crystal ball, or the wizard roaming his massive stone sanctum chanting incantations and extracting from the heavens prophecies of doom and disaster.

This is a vision so deeply ingrained that regardless of how intellectually superior we think we have become, our attitude towards the astrologer is still powerfully influenced by these stereotypes. Why else would so many otherwise sane and rational people have sat before me — the astrologer — as if they were at the dentist's about to be drilled, or at the doctor's awaiting a life or death prognosis? Or why did they come at all when, from the moment they walked in, their demeanour implied: 'I don't believe a word you're going to say!'?

Because they *do* believe. They *do* fear the supernatural, and the powers of the astrologer to foretell their fate, or read their darkest secrets.

Even the scoffers — perhaps they most of all — beneath their sophisticated, intellectual condemnations are prey to the same superstitious belief. Why else would they so strongly negate the validity of astrology without ever having the courage to test it for themselves? Or if they do make the effort, why do they judge it with such a narrow and biased set of rules that only proves their already established opinions rather than raise a true and open question about the subject? It does seem foolish, if consistent, to condemn anything at all that has qualities that render it beyond rational explanation by our present knowledge, especially given our past record in such matters. (No such thing as round worlds; the Earth is the centre of the solar system; human beings will fall apart if they travel beyond a certain speed; humans will never fly ...) Humankind's perennial conceit!

As for the seven-year-old oracle back in the playground thirty-five years ago, she was absolutely delighted with all the attention. Momentarily, she was a star. It did not occur to her that it might be harmful to hand out 'destinies' in such a loose and careless way — not that those particular prophecies would have held any threat ... though who knows who might have carried the suggestion of a business failure in their subconscious and unwittingly fulfilled it later on!

There is no doubt that the clients of astrologers generally credit them with more authority than they are entitled to, and it is clearly risky for a person to put him or herself in such a position. Astrologers too are only human and are no less affected by the energy of the symbol of power and authority their 'occult status' confers on them, and lures them to identify with. The consequence is that many of them reinforce this association, never suspecting that they are merely living up to what their public has come to expect. Many astrologers even capitalise on it, imagining they have magical access to the secret knowledge of the cosmos. One only has to look at the media's presentation of astrologers — particularly at the pseudonyms they are encouraged to adopt. (Bernadine Borealis and Madame Cosmos may not exist, but such aliases would not be exaggerations of those commonly in use.) One can only wonder if such individuals are not under some delusion about their identities.

There are, of course, those who do this purely for the fun of it, or with tongue in cheek. But there are undoubtedly those who take their cosmic aliases, and the role of prophet or soothsayer that goes with them, quite seriously.

And we encourage it. Because we want to believe. We want to have our fortunes told, however much we may deny it. We want the security of a known future — preferably filled with fame, wealth and happiness — because it is human nature to do so. The questions: '... will I be happy ... rich ... loved ... successful?' have not changed in hundreds of years. And neither has our understanding of astrology. We may not care to admit it but we, like our prehistoric ancestors, still need mediators to help us bridge the gap between the world we can see and the world we cannot. Our *shamans* may differ from their primitive counterparts in style and intent but their function as go-betweens has not changed.

There are those who, because they have scientific training and academic licence, legitimately stand as bridges between the conscious and rational world we know and the unconscious and irrational forces of the mind and body about which we are ignorant and wary. But it does not matter whether they are medical doctors, clergy, psychoanalysts, clairvoyants or astrologers. Anyone who can provide contact with the realms that lie beyond the boundaries of our personal knowledge and understanding serves this apparently indispensable office.

The psychologist translates dream symbols. In this way he or she helps patients understand, and in so doing contribute to, the changes occurring in their subconscious minds. This parallels the astrologer's translation of the symbols in clients' horoscopes. Both perform a type of psychological surgery which, because it can be seen only by its effects, is closer to the arcane than the scientific. This makes some people suspicious of both groups. However, psychology would naturally be more acceptable to those who are on the borderline.

There are many astrologers who concentrate on social and psychological problems. Usually they are trying to break free of its occult connotations, as well as of the overzealous religious interpretations that have been gradually woven into the structural principles of astrology. Their efforts to create a scientifically respectable image for this subject helps to make this service, once provided by our primitive medicine men, palatable to the tastes of the pragmatist and sceptic.

There is still a type of magic going on in these apparently respectable interchanges. In Jungian psychology, the resultant changes occurring in the psyche (of both healer and healed) are even referred to as 'alchemical'. But instead of black cats, steaming cauldrons and eye of newt; and rather than spells, curses and materialisations, the astrologer — like the psychologist — uses symbols. These images represent philosophical ideas and mythological archetypes, and they bridge the chasm between matter and spirit. For example, Mars is the God of War, — symbolising aggression, drive, anger; and Venus is the Goddess of Love, symbolising beauty, culture, human relations. To each person, each symbol has a general as well as a special and intimate meaning which transcends the intellect and reaches deep into the soul. The horoscope wheel itself is a symbol: it is a mandala — an instrument for focusing and integrating all the other symbols (and therefore the energies of the person concerned) into a cohesive whole.

Superstition cannot be despatched with the intellect. It is a formidable power which, at its worst, can undermine and even paralyse people's wills to take the initiative and responsibility for their lives. Astrology can be a valid and effective way of keeping the magic in our lives, while minimising the undesirable effects of superstition.

2 ORGINS

... *the failure to comprehend the present arises ineluctably from ignorance of the past* ...

MARC BLOCH, THE HISTORIAN'S CRAFT (APOLOGIE POUR L'HISTOIRE)

To understand how it all began, we are, for a moment going to take a trip back to our primitive roots, where our prehistoric ancestors related to their external world with their senses and instincts rather than with their intellects.

During these times humankind's continued existence depended very much on living in harmony with Nature's cyclic patterns. Consequently, their relationship with their environment was a tight and highly integrated one. They observed their world very carefully until, gradually, after countless aeons they began to notice that events not only occurred in a linear sequence but were also interrelated at each moment in time. In other words, they noticed the link between the changes going on around them and the changes in their own bodies and lives. All the connections were gradually made, remembered, and eventually notated.

There is evidence that around 35,000 years ago Cro-Magnon man recorded the phases of the Moon on the antlers of reindeer. To primitive man, birth and, therefore, woman, must have been the deepest mystery of all. Because the Moon's phases were seen to be connected with the human female cycle, it was regarded as a symbol of fertility and deep magic — a great mother goddess, a power to be feared, revered, and duly worshipped. From these beliefs evolved the first religions.

The Sun, too, was recognised as a great power and similarly deified. All over the world, ideas in the form of myths and legends became associated with the events of its rising and setting, its seasonal variations and its effects on life.

Connections between other heavenly phenomena with worldly events were also eventually made. In Egypt, for example, each year when the Nile rose and flooded its banks, bringing fertility and prosperity to the land and its people, a particularly bright star — Sirius — was observed to rise on the eastern horizon just ahead of the Sun.

Eclipses, supernovae and comets, being rare, were easily interpreted as portents of doom and, to the simpler minds of those times, threatening incidents. Eventually, five of the planets in our solar system (Mercury, Venus, Mars, Jupiter and Saturn) were discovered moving across the sky against a backdrop of stars that were soon to be constellated into the symbols of the zodiac.

The zodiac is the circle, or belt, of 'space' extending some nine degrees either side of the Sun's apparent path around the Earth. This path is called the ecliptic. Each of the twelve constellations, or groups of stars known as the signs of the zodiac (there are, of course, many other constellations in the skies), falls across the ecliptic so that the Sun and all the other planets in our solar system appear to us to pass through each one of them in turn. (It is, of course, the Earth that is moving and causing the Sun and planets to appear to move.) This circle, which is, strictly speaking, an ellipse, is divided equally into twelve segments of thirty degrees, and the Sun takes approximately one calendar month to pass through each sign. The amount of time spent in each sign by the other planets varies according to their respective distances from the Sun. The origin of the symbols (the ram for Aries, bull for Taurus, and so on) is obscure but, according to Richard Hinckley Allen in his *Star Names, Their Lore and Meeting*, it was 'in Euphratean astronomy'.

Everywhere, edifices — beginning with the simple standing stones of Europe and continuing through to such megalithic monuments as Stonehenge, the Great Pyramid of Cheops, the temples of Egypt and the pyramids of the Aztecs and Mayas — were slowly being erected. Opinions differ as to precisely why these monuments were erected but many presume that they were to assist in the study of the cosmos.

The transition from a Moon-ruled matriarchal society, which was wholly governed by superstition and fear through its strong link with the forces of darkness, to a Sun-ruled patriarchal society where reason and order (and science) prevailed, occurred in Egypt during the third millennium B.C. This roughly corresponds with the appearance of writing (3200 B.C.) and with the earliest authenticated records of astrology.

Obviously, astrology did not suddenly appear in a complete form. It must have been evolving for some time before it was organised into a structured scheme, and documented. In fact, it is generally accepted that it was in use for thousands of years prior to this date, but seemingly inseparable from other forms of divination — predominantly the use of omens. For example, it is recorded that one (unnamed) king summoned his astrologer/ diviner when a yellow dog entered the palace one day. The king took this to be an omen and wanted his astrologer to explain what it portended for the king and his subjects.

During its early days, astrology was used only to predict the future of nations and countries, rather than as a reference for individuals and their personal lives. Kings and rulers, however, were the exceptions, because it was considered that everything a king did was of great significance for his whole kingdom. Consequently, hardly a move was made without first consulting the court diviner or astrologer. In another example, a king asked his astrologer/priest whether he should receive the crown prince on his own or whether the prince should be accompanied by his attendants.

But the fame and notoriety of astrologers did not grow out of such apparently everyday interpretations. They were often able to predict major events, such as eclipses of the Sun and Moon, the outcome of wars and the onset of famines or plagues. The power to foresee at least some of these occurrences must have been awe-inspiring to the highly superstitious people of those times. And for their part, many astrologers flagrantly cultivated the reputation of supernatural power they engendered — as some of them still do.

But there is a price to pay for such power and many astrologers paid dearly for their claims. Some of them suffered ugly deaths when they were unable to prevent the eclipses they predicted — or any ensuing cataclysms. Clearly, these men led precarious lives, not only from the necessity of keeping their reputations and skins intact, but from other much more mundane perils. There is a story about the famous Greek scholar/astrologer Thales, who lived in an era when astrological reference material was not available. Accordingly, those learned men who consulted the star positions for guidance had to observe the skies personally each night in order to follow the planetary movements. Thales was duly pacing the countryside one dark night, watching the stars to see what the future had in store, when he fell down a well. (These were merely holes in the ground in those days and there were many of them dotted around the countryside.)

It is worth noting that, for all their alleged powers, many of these prophets were apparently powerless when it came to determining their own fate. Perhaps they were too busy with matters of state. Or perhaps they did not in those days, according to the custom, make their own horoscopes — though this is hard to believe, even taking into account that there is no evidence of personalised horoscopes before the fifth century B.C.

This was not an excuse that could have been used by Nektanebos, court astrologer to the parents of Alexander the Great, who lived during the fourth century B.C. The story goes that Nektanebos was present at the bedside of Olympias during her confinement and would not allow her to give birth to Alexander until the most propitious moment. Power indeed! This is amply demonstrated in the rest of the tale when, finally, Nektanebos gave the word and Alexander came forth to the accompaniment of thunder, lightning and earthquakes.

The vision of Nektanebos standing at the queen's window, commanding her to wait until he could see that all the planets were aligned in the proper manner is, not to be too disrespectful, a comical one. Apparently Alexander was none too impressed either. It seems that this astrologer's awesome powers declined as time went by, for when Alexander was 12 he decided that astrology was rubbish and to prove this pushed the unsuspecting foreteller off a wall. As walls in those times usually surrounded cities or fortresses, they must have been of considerable height, and Nektanebos died as a result of the fall. Another mark against predictive astrology and the infallible sorcerous powers attributed to astrologers!

Since the sixth century B.C., the Pythagoreans had been developing astrology along with magic and, at the same time, with mathematics. This combination would be enough to give our scientists the horrors. Astronomers too would be equally offended by the way in which astronomy and astrology were once fused together.

They consider their science the mother of all sciences and view astrology as an embarrassing relative. But this does not alter the fact that the term 'astronomy' was at one stage used to describe astro-meteorology — or, how the planets and stars affect the weather. This would be construed nowadays as a mystical matter. On the other hand, back in those days, 'astrology' also referred to the purely mathematical calculation of the stars for the purpose of navigation — which is today considered a scientific matter.

In the third century B.C. a form of astrology combined with medicine began to evolve. Called 'iatromathematics', it correlated the parts of the body, its illnesses and the appropriate medicinal remedies, with astrology. Incidentally, the symbol of the caduceus, associated with the medical profession to this day, is also connected in astrology with Mercury — the planet associated primarily with health.

As the Roman Empire grew, it adopted the more impressive beliefs of those countries it absorbed, astrology being one of those beliefs. The lower classes took to it very quickly but the upper echelons held back for a while. Unfortunately for their reputations, women accepted it immediately and were relentlessly ridiculed for it — as they still are.

During this early period astrology was on a roller-coaster ride through Roman history as its popularity rose and fell. It was condemned outright by many, yet upheld to the point of fanaticism by others. It was prostituted for status and power. It was denounced by many emperors openly while at the same time they used it to pinpoint those who might try to usurp their thrones. It was followed to the letter in the most petty matters, such as taking a bath or going to market.

Meanwhile, in Greece the Stoics were infusing it with their belief that fate was inescapable and predestined and that one should therefore face one's trials with courage and acceptance.

This notion of fatalism did a good deal of damage to astrology's acceptance in later times and has stuck fast even up to the present.

In the first century A.D. the great scholar Ptolemy (Claudius Ptolemaeus) compiled the *Tetrabiblos*. This was the first major reference for astrologers, consisting of all the astrological knowledge and information that had been accumulated up to that time. It became the central reference and authority for centuries to come and forms what is a sound, if rigid, basis for most of our present-day astrology.

The great naturalist, Pliny, who also lived in the first century A.D., incorporated astrological thought into all his varied subjects including, most interestingly, music. Pliny was not the first to do this, even at such an early date. The Pythagoreans before him (in the sixth century B.C.) believed in the existence of a universal harmony that was expressed by numbers and applicable to every part of life. In applying this to their musical scale, they found it to be in a straightforward numerical ratio. They believed, according to Aristotle, that the planets also 'produced different tones which we cannot hear because we have become so accustomed to them'. Consequently they applied this theory to the planetary positions and found that the circles the planets described in their revolutions in the heavens were in 'harmonious proportion to one another'. According to Colin Ronan in his extremely interesting *Changing Views of the Universe*, Pliny claimed the planetary intervals were as follows: the Earth and Mars, a whole tone; the Moon, Mercury and Jupiter, a semitone; Sun and Saturn, a minor third. (The remaining planets, Uranus, Neptune and Pluto were not known in Pliny's time.)

Also in the first century A.D., astrology in Greece was being separated from the main body of mathematics and was taking on a much more mystical form. Yet, paradoxically, it was allying itself more closely with medicine, which suggests that either medicine was less scientific or astrology was more so. About three centuries later, in Rome, philosophy and religion were also being combined with astrological principles.

In another part of the world, in the fifth century A.D., lived the probably mythical but nonetheless legendary character who contributed more than any other — with the possible exceptions of Nostradamus (Michel de Notredame, 1503–66) and, in more recent times, the great English astrologer-magician, Aleister Crowley (1875–1947) to our present image of the astrologer. This was, of course, the great magician Merlin. To him we probably owe not only our classic caricature of wizardry, but also the idea that astrology and magic are inextricably bound together. Whether or not this is a good thing, the legends surrounding King Arthur and Merlin, although shrouded in a cloak of mystical symbolism, have stimulated a lot of interest today. And the study of these legends and myths has led to an insight into the symbols that the unconscious mind uses and which are manifested in our dreams.

Merlin's connection with astrology naturally damaged the subject because of his link with black magic. Such 'demonic and sorcerous adjuncts' (as one medieval detractor puts it) were, and still are, unacceptable to Christian ethics. And the fate and favour of astrology grew to be more and more dependent on the view taken by the Church.

Further doubt was thrown upon the validity of astrology by an Egyptian Christian sect, the Copts, in the fifth century A.D. Their doctrines and beliefs were based upon a claimed discovery of records that had been written during the life of Jesus Christ — allegedly *after* his recorded departure from this earth. According to these claims, Christ lived on and began a new life in some other part of the world.

These records also state that when Jesus ascended to heaven after his death, he passed through the realm of the five planetary gods, the Archons, and weakened them. This caused them to become confused in their influence so that astrologers, who were seen to be worshipping false gods rather than the one true God, would from then on have difficulty in predicting with any consistent accuracy. The aim of this was to give them cause to reflect upon the error of their ways. One can only assume that the Archons have not yet been able to unravel their lines of communication with astrologers. One cannot help but be grateful for this, for it is a lifeline which the victim of astrological malpractice can grab when predictions of illness, death or other misfortune are carelessly made.

As philosophical and religious thought grew, so too did occultism. The first five books of the Old Testament came to be most influential and thought-provoking. They in fact became the basis of the *Kabbalah* — a work associated with modern-day Tarot and numerology. Unfortunately the philosophical and spiritual ideals contained in this famous work were gradually smothered as, along with astrology, they fell slowly beneath the inexorable press of distorted occultism.

During this period it appears that astrologers were more or less split into three main groups: those whose interest in astrology was purely academic; those whose main aim was to gain personal power; and those who were seeking only to develop the spirit. However, Christianity continued to deplore its use and throughout medieval times at least, the Church officially condemned it. Nonetheless, this did not stop some of the Church's representatives from continuing to practise the art.

In the thirteenth century, Thomas Aquinas, one of the great theologians of the Roman Catholic Church, helped to improve astrology's image by emphasising the fact that the stars governed only the senses. He believed that if man was able to rise above his animal nature he would be beyond the reach of his 'star destiny'. This precept has weathered the storms of ensuing centuries and is still strongly adhered to in certain schools of astrological thought.

Later, in the fifteenth century, a Dominican called Ficino, who was revered as a great scholar, also studied and practised astrology. Unfortunately for him he included in his studies subjects that were even more questionable and generally regarded as superstitious nonsense. He and his kind were abused caustically by the intelligentsia of his time and were labelled 'drivelling and evil' idiots — a sentiment no doubt shared by many sceptics today.

Whatever the accusations against him, there is no denying Ficino's scholastic prowess and his extreme devotion to his work, so his contribution to astrology cannot be ignored. One particular category to which he contributed greatly was that of cosmogenical music. He composed musical themes to encourage the effects of benevolent planetary influences, which would in turn offset the effects of bad ones.

He believed that music expressed emotion perfectly and that each planet represented a particular sphere of emotion. Venus represented peace, gaiety and love; Mars was anger and aggression; Saturn, coldness and austerity. It must have been a fascinating field, into which even the famed astronomer Kepler was lured. Johann Kepler (1571–1630) calculated mathematically the musical tones of each planet, based on their orbital velocities. On the basis of this it would seem feasible that a horoscope could be expressed by a single chord made up of all the various notes or tones derived from the positions of the planets in their relationship to each other. Perhaps even a symphony of life could be composed from the changing tones resulting from the planets moving on their individual courses through the heavens. It would in fact be surprising if this has not been attempted.

Despite the strong interest in and study of astrology by scholarly and respected men during the fifteenth and sixteenth centuries, many who dared to challenge the established order of life as set down by the Church were tortured or burned at the stake.

Although astronomy was, according to some sources, not yet subject to quite such drastic reactions, the astronomer Copernicus (1473–1543) was greatly concerned about his reputation when he rediscovered the validity of an astronomical system which claimed that the Sun, rather than the Earth, was at the centre of the Universe — this was the Heliocentric system. He produced his work *The Revolutions of the Celestial Orbs* over a number of years prior to 1530, but dared not have it published for many years because he greatly feared ridicule. Finally he succumbed to the encouragement of friends, and eventually even of the Church, and it was finally published in 1543. The story is that he received a copy on his deathbed, too ill even to know what it was, and was therefore unable to detect that it was not set from his original manuscript, a fact that was not discovered until the nineteenth century in Prague. Why this deception occurred is not known. However, given the increasing rigidity of the Church's views and laws at that time, it is feasible to speculate that it might have been tampered with to make it less threatening to the Church's established order. It was discovered that the Preface of the published book was not original, and modified the claims made by Copernicus about his 'new' vision of the universe, and the Earth's much less prominent part in it.

Despite the popularity of the old Earth-centred, or Geocentric, system, the great scientists Tycho Brahe, Kepler, Galileo, and others, slowly disproved it. They could not avoid doing so as the increasing number of facts revealed by their astronomical advances weighed more and more heavily on the side of reality.

The Church might have been quick to condemn astrology, but some popes nonetheless continued to use it for their own, often nefarious, purposes. One of Galileo's friends was the Dominican Pope, Urban VIII. This esteemed and venerated personage, with the aid of the Italian philosopher, poet and writer, Campanella, had horoscopes cast for the cardinals of Rome and then had their deaths publicly predicted. However, as was the inclination of many in high office who indulged in this habit, when other astrologers began predicting his own imminent death he quickly passed a new law stating that any astrologers who predicted the deaths of princes, popes, or any members of their families, would be executed.

However, in order to dispel the effects of the eclipse from which was predicted his own death, Urban procured the assistance of Campanella. Together they went into seclusion to carry out the necessary rites that were supposed to counteract the prediction. The following description of these rites illustrates the diversity of astrological influence at that time most aptly.

First they sealed the room against the outside air, sprinkled it with rose-vinegar and other aromatic substances, and burnt laurel, myrtle, rosemary and cypress. They hung the room with white silken cloths and decorated it with branches. Then two candles and five torches were lit, representing the seven planets; since the heavens, owing to the eclipse, were defective, these were to provide an undefective substitute, as one lights a lamp when the sun sets. The signs of the Zodiac were perhaps also

*represented in the same way; for this is a philosophical procedure, not a
superstitious one, as common people think. The other persons present
had horoscopes immune to the evil eclipse. There was Jovial [Jupiterian]
and Venereal [Venusian] music, which was to disperse the pernicious
qualities of the eclipse-infected air and, by symbolising good planets, to
expel the influences of bad ones. For the same purpose they used stones,
plants, colours and odours, belonging to the good planets (that is, Jupiter
and Venus). They drank astrologically distilled liquors.*

(D.P. WALKER,
SPIRITUAL AND DEMONIC MAGIC FROM FICINO TO CAMPANELLA)

Here you can see the extent to which the planets were given
rulership over all the fields of life: herbs, talismans, stones,
colours, smells, music, clothes, temperature, air, water, wines
and people — all were summoned to assist in the task of evading
a person's predicted fate.

So much of the astrologer's time during this period must
have been taken up with mathematical computations that it is
almost a wonder he was ever able to apply his results in practice.
The more he learned about the heavens, the more complex
matters became for him. Before too long, fortunately, mathematical tables were developed so that it became less necessary
for the astrologer to be an astronomer and a mathematician.
This meant that he had more time to concentrate on the effects
and meanings of astrology.

Catherine de Medici's personal astrologer was the now
popular, then notorious, Nostradamus. Many of the predictions
astrologers were commissioned by royalty to make turned out
to be very different from what the regal petitioner had in mind.
As in earlier times, it was dangerous work, particularly when
patronised by those in high office as in Nostradamus's case. In
fact, Nostradamus appears to have written his prophecies in
such an obscure manner that it is believed it was a diplomatic
move to avoid being persecuted.

However, he did, on at least one crucial occasion, neglect his
precautions. In agreement (some say) with another astrologer,
Nostradamus openly and plainly predicted the death of Henry II
in single combat, omitting none of the gory details. The prophecy

was fulfilled and Henry II died such a horrible death that society became infuriated with Nostradamus, whom they blamed, saying that he used magic to make his prediction come true. Catherine de Medici adamantly defended him but ironically, from then only his magic kept him from ignominy. Once again, the wizard image was reinforced.

Shortly after this came the final parting between astrology and astronomy. When Galileo constructed his first telescope in 1609, revealing a vast new field of astronomical data, astronomy had little choice but to take a more specialised and scientific path. Astrology's fate was more or less sealed by this movement, for its dignity and plausibility were also being undermined further by corruption. The academic factions that had for so long contributed to the respectability of astrology were steadily withdrawing their sanction and, released from its academic tethers and support, astrology was quickly gobbled up by the occultists and metaphysicians.

However, despite this demoralisation there were still a few altruists in the astrological field who tried to uphold the higher principles of the art. One of these was the English astrologer, William Lilly (1602–81) whose famous *Epistle to the Student of Astrology* is often quoted in astrological circles. The high standards he attempted to set are clearly seen in the following extract.

> ... the more thy knowledge is enlarged, the more doe thou magnify the power and wisdome of Almighty God; strive to preserve thyself in his favour; for the more holy thou art, and more neer to God, the purer judgment thou shalt give.
>
> Beware of pride and self-conceit: remember how that long agoe no irrationall creature durst offend man the Macrocosme, but did faithfully serve and obey him; so long as he was master of his own reason and passions, or until he subjected his will to the unreasonable part ... Doe not, then, for shame deface thy nature ... As thou daily conversest with the heavens, so instruct and form thy mind according to the image of Divinity: learn all the ornaments of virtue ... be humane, curtius, familiar to all, easie of accesse: afflict not the miserable with terrour of a harsh judgment; direct such to call on God, to divert his judgments

impending over them: be civil, sober, covet not an estate; give freely to
the poor, both money and judgment: let no worldly wealth procure an
erronious judgment from thee, or such as may dishonour the art …

Lilly was also famous for his predictions. In 1651 he
predicted the Great Plague and Great Fire of 1665 and 1666
respectively. It is an indication of the animosity felt for astrologers
at that time that he was, like Nostradamus, actually accused by
a tribunal of having started the fire himself to make his prediction
come true.

And then, of course, there was Sir Isaac Newton, whose
contributions to science formed the foundations of our more
recent physical reach to the stars. A very famous statement of
his, made to the astronomer Halley in the course of a discussion
on astrology, is often resorted to as a defence by astrology's
adherents: 'The difference between you and me … is that I
have studied the subject and you have not!'

Whether Newton believed in astrology or not is uncertain.
But if he did support it, he cannot be blamed for being close-
mouthed about the fact, for as the eighteenth century drew nearer,
astrology seems to have reached its nadir. Around the rapidly
diminishing hard core of the serious, scholastically inclined
astrologer was growing a veneer of mystification, created mainly
by unprincipled sects bent on using astrology, among other
mystical arts, for selfish and nefarious purposes. These groups
comprised the vanguard of the irresistible drift of astrology
towards magic and trickery. As commercial art, these crafts
were becoming all the rage. However, even magicians, who
had at least commanded considerable respect in earlier times,
were now considered mere conjurers.

At about the same time that the commercialisation of magic
and various other 'occult' practices came about, there grew a
very strong interest in intellectualism for its own sake. The
outcome of this, along with the rapid advance of pure science,
was that astrology did not qualify as being acceptable under
this newly found 'understanding' of reality, and was denounced
as delusion and charlatanism. Unfortunately this was probably

accurate in many instances. In fact, charlatanism in these fields was so prevalent that the British Government once again stepped in and, in the Vagrancy Acts of 1824–98, decreed that those 'deceiving the King's Subjects by purporting to tell fortunes or draw up horoscopes' should be punished by law. Until the 1930s, astrologers and others whose activities came under the classification of the Act were arrested, fined, and even imprisoned.

As we draw closer to the present in this historical outline, some sects practising astrology began to lean once more towards a spiritual view, concentrating on the idea of a soul in perpetual reincarnation. This particular shift was brought about by the Theosophists, who were attempting to bring Eastern philosophies and spiritual ideologies to the Western mind.

This met with some difficulty when theosophical ideas clashed with certain traditional astrological beliefs, such as the rigid, mechanical, fatalistic type of dogmas which had been accepted for so many centuries. The Theosophists' idea that man could rise above his fate 'as laid down by the stars' was basically high-minded and idealistic. However, there was still a tendency to interpret the various indications in horoscopes as rigidly 'good' or 'evil'. Although some slight awareness that this black and white approach to horoscope interpretation was not a true one did filter through, there seemed to be few who could actually see and predict any shades between Shangri-la and purgatory.

On the other hand, also in the late nineteenth and early twentieth centuries, there still existed astrologers whose reputations were such that their astrology too fell under the dark mantle of 'black magic' and charlatanism. Such a one was Aleister Crowley, whose philosophy was the fundamentally spiritual ideal of the elimination of separativeness by destroying 'self' (getting rid of 'I'). Unfortunately, his methods of accomplishing what he described as 'the supreme achievement' were so radical and scandalous at the time they earned him the title of 'the apocalyptic Beast' — which in the end he himself claimed to be.

This brings us to the present, where, despite our proud late twentieth century self-awareness, we are still having great difficulty in breaking this habit. Astrology's omen-oriented roots are just too deeply embedded and we can expect to wait a long time for a true mutation of our instinctive reaction to astrology and its practitioners.

Nonetheless, astrology has advanced tremendously in the past 10 to 15 years alone. It has led a chameleon-like existence all through history and is yet again adapting, with its usual dexterity, to the needs and whims of the times. Regardless of how much it may be outlawed by science, astrology has always added other dimensions to our understanding of ourselves and our lives and it will probably continue to do so.

3 ASTROLOGY AND SCIENCE

Science and mysticism are polar opposites. The intellect or conscious mind needs logical reasons. It needs a structured framework within which the unknown can be safely imprisoned and thereby rendered harmless. It wants all the mysteries of life reduced to controllable and neatly labelled facts so that life can be orderly: the intellect's version of security. The development of science is a natural extension of these needs.

Mysticism, which instinctively accepts the unknown and its symbols, is the natural extension of the unconscious mind.

But no human being is purely mind, or purely instinct; purely scientific or purely mystical.

The scientist is driven to know 'why', and there can be as much passion and fervour on the trail of a discovery as in a religious gathering. Many major breakthroughs are in fact the result of a final grand intuitive leap beyond logic. When such an instantaneous perception occurs, the ordered and logical sequence of steps — the pieces of the pattern — are drawn together into a cohesive whole far greater than the sum of all the individual parts. Clearly, intuition and the unconscious mind are an integral part of the victories of science.

There are many stories about scientists who have experienced such a meeting of the conscious and unconscious mind in a moment of vivid awareness. There is the chemist who actually felt physically uncomfortable — as if his shoes were pinching him — when confronted with molecular models that were 'too tightly packed'. Friedrich Kekulé — also a chemist — after a long period of intense study and experiment had sudden visions in his mind's eye of dancing atoms coming together in their proper patterns and sequences. Henri Poincaré, a mathematician, when pondering mathematical formulae in a drowsy reverie, was confronted with an image of the formulae combining and recombining in their proper mathematical classes.

Science and astrology both attempt to describe, classify and organise certain phenomena in an effort to bring a sense of order and meaning into our lives. The main difference is that they both approach this goal from opposite points.

Science starts out with the parts — a list of facts — and uses intuition to grasp the essence of the whole that those combined parts make. Astrology starts out with an act of intuitive faith, an instinctive acceptance of what the subconscious perceives instantaneously in 'wholes'. Then, through the language of the symbols of the horoscope, it uses logic to break the whole up into parts in order to define them (the horoscope is the individual; the horoscope is made up of planets and their relationships with each other; a particular planet represents and describes the individual's drive, goals, and so on).

Although intuition undoubtedly plays the major part in astrological interpretation, the astrologer has also to base this on concrete data, mathematical formulae and planetary position as well as on direct experience, observation, and the knowledge of how the components behaved previously and repeatedly — in much the same way as scientific understanding and knowledge develops.

It must be made quite clear at this juncture that my aim here is not to try to prove astrology — least of all with the often misguided method some astrologers use in pointing out that, if this scientific principle is like that astrological one, then astrology must be science. There are certainly some dramatic correlations between the two, which I intend to present, but as food for thought only.

ENERGY

Energy is at the basis of everything that exists: light, sound, heat, matter, and so on. Matter — the very stuff of our lives — may be solid to our senses but in fact consists of 'concentrated bundles of energy', as one school physics text puts it.

Naturally enough, we take this hidden energy for granted. We cannot see the endless activity going on within the atoms of a piece of furniture or a rock, the constant movement of the elementary particles as they are driven by a continuous attraction and repulsion — an activity known as electromagnetism. Whether a substance is a solid, liquid or gas depends on how fast these elementary particles are vibrating.

Everything in our world — solid, liquid or gas, colour and light, and anything else you can think of, is really a conglomeration of vibrating particles, radiating energy in the form of electromagnetic waves.

Most of the electromagnetic spectrum is outside the capacity of our senses and only a very narrow range is visible to us as light. These waves vary in frequency according to their wavelength. The shorter the wavelength, the higher the frequency transmitted.

A human being is also a 'transmitter' in the sense that his or her molecules are vibrating and therefore emitting electromagnetic radiation, albeit very slight. Some of these frequencies can of course be measured by instruments such as the electroencephelograph which measures brainwave frequencies.

Human beings are also 'receivers' and are under a constant barrage from everything around us, both within and outside the Earth's atmosphere. For example, in recent years light waves have been discovered to have a far deeper physical effect than had previously been imagined. Via the photoreceptors of the eye, and the optic nerve, these rays stimulate specific glands to produce certain hormones and suppress others. This is vital to the regulation and synchronisation of our complex and delicately tuned biological systems.

As our solar system speeds through space it passes through a constant barrage of cosmic radiations from many other sources too. Our atmosphere filters and reflects many of these radiations, yet we have only to observe the effects of the Sun's rays alone on our physical world to wonder what less obvious effects other radiations might be having on our own 'oscillating particles'.

Then there are sound waves. Sound waves cannot travel through space. They need an atmosphere, a substance, a medium through which to travel in order to produce pressure on the eardrum — or other 'energy converter'.

An intriguing aspect of sound waves is their ability to elicit a response in other objects. Experiments with tuning forks show that the pitch of two forks can be adjusted to coincide so that if one fork is struck, it will cause the other to vibrate — or resonate in synchronisation.

Sound is not the only energy capable of producing resonance. Each substance and object is composed of vibrating particles, as noted previously, and has its own particular vibratory frequency. Within a prescribed distance, any two substances, or bodies, can 'resonate' to each other in the same way that tuning forks do — though not because of sound waves.

In their fascinating book, *The Cycles of Heaven*, Guy Lyon Playfair and Scott Hill investigate thoroughly, and without occult interest or allusion, the effect of cosmic forces on human beings. They examine closely scientific research into the concept of 'music of the spheres' — 'music' in this context implying an interchange of energies resulting in resonance caused by something other than sound. In fact, this theory has been investigated exhaustively since the Pythagoreans first connected music with mathematics several thousand years ago. Playfair and Hill suggest that the planetary rates of vibration (their wavelength frequencies) are so low — something like one cycle per day, or even as little as one cycle per year — that we cannot possibly be aware of them. However, this does not mean that they do not in some way affect us, just as certain sound frequencies below (infrasonic) or above (ultrasonic) what we can hear, affect us.

Playfair and Hill's research produced information that strongly suggested energy exchanges do occur between certain heavenly bodies. For example, the Earth and Venus are involved in an interchange of energies as a result of a regularly repeated relationship between them. This relationship occurs as Venus shows the same face to the Earth whenever Venus is between the Earth and the Sun.

These 'resonances', which are produced gravitationally, result from the different angular relationships between planets as they move along their paths around the Sun. In astrology, certain of the angles they make between each other are invested with the power of producing influences on the energy levels of human beings.

One astrologer (Stephen Arroyo) has likened these angular relationships to electrical theory. In electrical wiring systems, the best way of conducting energy is to use a three-phase current at 120° spacing. If 90° or 180° spacing is used, it results in overheating because the energy is transmitted along the wire unevenly; that is, it travels in short bursts rather than in an uninterrupted flow.

This is precisely how astrologers have described — long before electricity was discovered — the influence of the angular relationships based on the division of the 360° zodiac circle by three (resulting in the 60° and 120° angles) and by four (resulting in the 90° and 180° angles). In fact, these are the primary angles used in astrology to describe individual character and experience. In other words, if planets are placed at 60° or 120° apart, the energy associated with this relationship between them is smooth and harmonious — usually 'easy' for an individual to control and direct. The 90° and 180° angles — and their derivatives — are, on the other hand, always interpreted as uneven spurts of energy. Astrology says that personal energies affected by the latter types of planetary relationships blow hot and cold and are more difficult to control. Usually they produce restlessness, irritability and rashness, depending on the planets concerned. These angles tend to result in the same sort of stress and overload on a person as on an electrical wiring system.

PATTERNS

The most significant correlations between the scientific world and the astrological one are found in the field of mathematics.

Scientist Charles-Noël Martin became fascinated with life's

fundamental patterns and published a book, *The Thirteen Steps to the Atom*, on this subject. The thirteen steps to which he refers are grades he gives to the various elements of life, ranging from the snowflake — which he places at the thirteenth step — to the smallest known particle — the 'elementary particle', which he puts at the first step. He photographed the world of this microcosm and showed the incredible geometrical order innate in this inner world. He says of these geometrical arrangements that '... molecules do not arrange themselves in random order or directions. *Remote forces come into play* and the groups of molecules take up positions dictated by these forces *and their own innate structure*'. (Emphasis added.) The most graphic examples of this are in the precise, repetitive patterns that occur within gemstones: the crystals of quartz and sapphires are of a triangular pattern; garnets are formed from isometric (cuboid) crystals; diamond crystals form in octahedrons, and so on.

At a more abstract level, this repetition of pattern persists: in Chinese and Indian philosophies the way in which our personal experiences and our collective evolution proceed corresponds with their concept of the spiralling serpent life force; and this is carried over into astrological principles. Spirals were also frequently used by prehistoric man in his markings on ancient standing stones. And we live in a spiral galaxy — a pattern repeated from this greatest entity of which we are a part, down to the microscopic DNA which dictates our genetic patterns.

TIDES

Tides are also involved in the creation of patterns. Not only do tidal pulls occur in oceans, they also occur in the atmosphere, in the plasma of space and of the Sun, as well as in bodily fluids. The ancient Chinese were well aware of this tidal effect in all aspects of life and they used the knowledge to enhance their lives, and also their healing methods. Their system of acupuncture, for example, is based on the ebb and flow of *chi*, or vital energy, along minutely defined pathways through the body.

Scientists are rediscovering this tidal or cyclical effect in the body and are developing new healing methods based on the ebb and flow of energies and chemicals in the body. One such method is 'chronobiology'. This particular science was born when it was found that if a drug is administered at a time of day when the bodily cycle connected with the diseased system is at a peak, the drug is considerably more effective.

Cycles and tides imply rhythm — a coming and a going. This rhythm is mirrored in Newton's Third Law of Motion which states that 'to every action force there is an equal and opposite reaction force'. The law was in fact discovered a long long time before Sir Isaac Newton's time. In India it was called the 'Law of Karma', or the law of cause and effect and it is not only a scientific criterion for the existence of life but is also fundamental to the basic tenets of astrology because it denotes the dynamic interaction that takes place between the cosmos and humanity. It describes humanity's actions and the way in which these actions set up 'waves' in the world around us (in the cosmos), which then flow back to us.

As an extension of this concept, in the preface to his book, *Astrology and Science*, French psychologist and statistician Michel Gauquelin refers to Charles-Noël Martin's table for establishing the 'thirteen gradations of the infinitely small', and puts forward the provocative theory that if we multiply the size of an elementary particle (estimated at one-thousandth of one-billionth of a millimetre) by the average human height (1.75 metres), we arrive at the — completely incomprehensible — figure of 1,750,000,000,000,000. This, he says, means that human beings can 'control' (by the act of moving a limb, for example) a particle that is 1,750,000,000,000,000 times smaller than themselves.

If we took this a step further and reversed the concept by considering a particle that same distance from the body *outwardly* in proportion to that distance *inwardly*, this would take us some 3220 billion kilometres (2000 billion miles) out into space. And if we can 'control', or at least affect, a particle 1,750,000,000,000,000 times distant from us inwardly, we could theoretically affect particles that many times distant from us outwardly, and perhaps those particles, or objects, could also affect us.

On this basis, the planet Pluto, which is to date the most distant object discovered in our solar system, is actually proportionally much closer to us than is an atom — an elementary particle — within our bodies. It is but a short step from this to the idea that we affect, and could be affected by, distant planets, or even stars or other objects that we would not ordinarily be aware of at all — and this in all directions! It opens up the possibility that the unique planetary configurations occurring at birth may be connected with specific energy formations that in turn create, or reflect, the unique genetic patterns of each human being. On this basis an astrologer could look at someone's horoscope and know if that person was prone to depression, for example, because that individual's chemical and hormonal make-up would be indicated by the patterns in the natal horoscope. This is in fact the way planetary influences are interpreted in medical astrology.

As far as astrological prediction goes, we could say that when a planet reaches a position coincident with that of a planet in the natal chart, the current or transiting planetary influence (energy) temporarily alters the original 'electro-chemical' pattern of that individual. In other words, we might say that the gravitational push and pull of the planets changes the vibration of the elementary particles in our bodies. This, in turn, changes the chemical and hormonal balance, which produces physical and psychological changes such as illness or mood swings. So all of this, and more, could be read as possibility in an individual's horoscope by observing the current relationships of the planets in the sky with the natal planetary positions.

Some branches of science, such as geophysics, meteorology and astronomy, have shown considerable interest in the effect of planetary relationships and earthquakes, weather upheavals and radio disturbances. Most of these investigations began because of the suspiciously coincidental correspondences between sunspot cycles (those approximately 11.1-year periodical bursts of solar activity) and earthquakes, major political and economic

upheavals, and climatic and radio disturbances. It appears that
there is a mounting interest among some scientists in the possibility of planetary and/or solar energies directly affecting the
human entity and our planet.

So far, however, it is clear that science has little or no
intention of giving leeway to astrology. Generally findings are
presented in a guarded manner so that there is no danger of
them being construed as being supportive of astrology. But
occasionally their own research turns scientists' ideas around.

This happened to Michel Gauquelin who wanted, in his
own words, 'to clear the humbug from astrology'. He collated
a mass of statistics derived from thousands of births. The results
of his surveys tended, in fact, to disprove many earlier 'statistical'
claims put forward by over-enthusiastic astrologers. Gauquelin's
research showed their data to be inadequate, variable, unreliable,
and therefore unacceptable as statistical evidence.

However, despite his own disbelief, one of his studies turned
up some convincing evidence *for* the case of astrology. Unfortunately, his work has been misrepresented by a few astrologers
who, misguidedly hoping to convince and prove astrology scientifically, succeeded only in damaging its reputation still further
because of their blatantly biased misuse of the data.

Although this statistical research did help astrology by
proving that it works — if not quite in the way astrologers
claimed — it nonetheless created more problems for its credi-
bility. In a statistical examination, only one factor is extracted
and monitored in each test. For example, one of the questions
Gauquelin asked was: 'How many times does Saturn appear
on the horizon or Midheaven at the time of death?'

This is wholly inadequate as a means of measuring such a
complex event. No single planetary position can account for
such a major event. Unfortunately, the fact that statistical
evidence *was* found in the study on vocations associated with
specific planetary positions, gave the false impression that a
single factor can be used for *all* statistical purposes.

There is no denying that in astrological interpretation the
planets do have their individual correspondences with affairs
of life. And the planet Saturn situated on the Midheaven — as

in Gauquelin's test — could certainly be associated with death in some instances. However, it could also, in this position, be associated with a career change: a demotion, or promotion. The effects for each person vary according to how each planet is placed in the birth horoscope — where it is placed, which area of life it influences the most, whether it is made stronger or weaker by its position; and how the other planets relate to it — not to mention all the current planetary placements. Many factors have to be taken into account and properly integrated for anything approaching an accurate and personal appraisal of their combined effect with such a position as 'Saturn on the Midheaven'.

THE CASE AGAINST ASTROLOGY AS A SCIENCE

Despite the possibility of astrology eventually being proven scientifically, there is one very damning fact which is invariably cited by astrology's adversaries and which leads many sceptics to deny the existence or validity of astrology.

The doubters argue that because of the way in which the Earth wobbles like a spinning top as it turns on its own axis, the actual zodiacal *constellations* in the sky are continually moving out of phase with the zodiacal signs. As the zodiac originally derived its meanings from the constellations, non-astrologers who know about the movement find it ludicrous that the same meanings are still given to areas of space that no longer have anything to do with those constellations.

What this means to the individual is that when astrologers say someone's Sun is in the sign of Aries, they are referring to its position in their zodiac — the 'Tropical Zodiac' (or the 'moving' zodiac), rather than to the 'Sidereal Zodiac' (the 'fixed' zodiac) used by astronomers. So if you were to make a simple observation of the heavens at that moment (assuming you were in the right place at the right time), you would plainly see that the Sun was not in the actual constellation of Aries at all but in that of Pisces.

This is because the Earth's poles rotate in a backward motion through the constellations (caused by the top-like wobble mentioned above). The movement, known as the 'precession of the equinoxes,' takes approximately 25,800 years to complete a full circle. In the time of Ptolemy — who supplied the Western world with perhaps the most significant astrological reference, being the first of its kind — the North Pole pointed towards the constellation of Aries at the Vernal Equinox (21 March), which is still taken as the beginning of our modern zodiac. At that time, however, when an astrologer said that the Sun was in Aries, it really was. Now, the North Pole points to the constellation of Pisces on 21 March each year. And this discrepancy will worsen because every 2150 years the Pole moves backwards another full sign. Before too long, a person born with the Sun in astrological Aries will astronomically have it in Aquarius because the Sun's true position in the sky will be almost two full signs away from its astrological position. (Many believe it has already entered Aquarius, which is why there is currently such an upsurge of worldwide interest in the 'Age of Aquarius'.)

A fact that would irritate the sceptics even more if they knew of it — and some do of course — is that Indian astrologers use this 'real' or actual astronomical zodiac, and they claim that their system is the correct one. Having had the opportunity to observe the Indian system of astrology in action, I am convinced that their system works too, even though the aforementioned differences between the bases on which the two systems are structured would make it logically impossible. Astrology, like many other matters, not least of all the inner world of the atom, does not always behave in a manner that accommodates the expectations and demands of logic or classic scientific laws. It behaves according to its own laws, which does not make it any less valid. It simply requires more careful research.

It may seem strange that those who uphold the enigmatic concept that the world is an illusion (which the Western mind generally has some difficulty in grasping) have a more scientific approach to their astrology than we do. But it could be that their use of a system founded on the true solar position in the actual constellations may be a counterbalance to their more mystical approach to life. And in beautiful symmetry, our system, which is based on an abstract idea rather than a physically observable reality, could similarly be a way of compensating for our strongly pragmatic world view.

Whatever the reasons, whether we are Eastern or Western, mystic or scientist, we are arriving more and more at the same conclusions about life. Ask the physicist chasing the ever-diminishing fundamental particle if life is the illusion that mystics have for centuries been claiming it is and, judging by comments made in the latest science journals and magazines, it would seem that there are an increasing number who are at least beginning to suspect that it is, and some agreeing with this outright. They are certainly making more frequent observations about the interdependence of life systems and life forms, implying that our lives and actions are inescapably interwoven into the patterns and cycles of our Earth. The Earth in turn slots into the cycles of the solar system, which may be interdependent on our galaxy, or the universe. Or in the words of the history and German literature scholar Erich Kahler (1885–1970) in his sensitive work, *The Meaning of History*: 'It may well be that all of us are unknowingly enmeshed in a vast coordinated coherence, just as a cell is unaware of the organism to which it belongs.'

Charles-Noël Martin says the same thing in another way:

> ... *All this serves to illustrate observations about the interpenetration of things and their dependence on, and solidarity with, their immediate and remote surroundings, down to the very atoms.*

(THIRTEEN STEPS TO THE ATOM)

As to the argument of whether astrology is or is not a science, I must agree that it does not, at this stage, fall within the parameters of science. Ironically, some scientists, such as astronomers and meteorologists, are closer than are most astrologers to proving inadvertently that planetary or cosmic relationships are linked to specific reactions on planet Earth — which is of course the crux of astrological rationale. (If science did ever happen to prove astrology there would undoubtedly still be a battle between the two factions about what and how.)

My own view, which is becoming increasingly reinforced,

is that the real question is not whether the stars or planets actually affect human beings, but rather, do such cosmic relationships reflect, that is, correspond with, the cycles and patterns we experience personally and collectively? Something along the lines of 'as above, so below' ... a question of simultaneity ... synchronicity ... matters we cannot yet comprehend in this context.

Either way, all we can do until we have more knowledge or more understanding is to continue with our investigations and accept astrology for what it is — or reject it for what it is not.

PART II
STRUCTURE

1 THE CYCLES
OF LIFE

The Chinese philosophical concept that the Universe consists of two main forces: yang and yin (active and passive, male and female, and so on) which constantly change into one another in a perpetual cyclic rhythm, has been accepted for thousands of years, and not only by the Chinese. Recently this idea was inadvertently given scientific support by the awesome genius of Stephen Hawking, an astro-physicist at Cambridge University, England, who with his colleague Jim Hartle, developed the mathematical theory that the Universe not only expands and contracts rhythmically and cyclically, but will do so eternally.

Everything in our known Universe — according to our limited perception — is a part of some greater or smaller cycle.

This apparently limitless and unequivocal Inbreath and Outbreath of the Universe is the greatest cycle of all.

Somewhere in the midst of this infinity spins our speck of a galaxy. In a tiny corner at the edge of this galaxy is our microscopic solar system, revolving rhythmically around the core of the galaxy.

Within these almost incomprehensibly huge cycles are smaller cycles with tempos we can recognise and which more noticeably affect us. The sunspot cycle, for instance, appears to affect, if not coincide with, fluctuations in our world and in our everyday lives. It has been suggested that this cycle affects earthquake activity, epidemics, tree rings, heart failure, weather, voting trends, the mortality rate and the flocculation of blood.

Then there is the Earth revolving annually around the Sun, producing the seasons, and within that cycle the Earth rotating on its own axis, causing night and day.

The human cycle of birth, life and death is regulated to within such an extraordinarily narrow time band that, in the context of the immeasurable reaches of time and space, it is astoundingly precise.

Finally, at the bottom of this graduated list of cycles are our personal cycles: physical, mental and emotional.

So, we have the rhythms of the universe; the galaxy, the solar system, the Sun, the Earth, the human race, and the organic rhythms within each individual being. Each system is an organism, complete within itself yet inextricably connected with all the others in an intricate and perfect coherence.

All of these systems ebb and flow, sometimes synchronising, sometimes counterpointing each other. In the same way, each of us enters into, meshes with, or polarises — and therefore changes in some way — not only the lives of others but also other organic systems.

The planets revolving around the Sun create interweaving relationships with each other and with the Sun. These relationships form patterns in time as well as in space. Our personal rhythms are as much a reflection of the rhythms and patterns of the universe as those of the universe are a reflection of ours (hardly a new thought). And your horoscope is a transcript of those patterns as they were at the moment of your birth. It marks the point at which you entered into the combined planetary cycles of our solar system — cycles which eventually merge with the greater galactic and universal ones.

The horoscope has always been regarded as a 'frozen moment in time' — a type of photographic still of our solar system from the point of view of the particular spot on Earth and the specific moment at which the entity concerned was born.

The cycles of the planets continue from that point, of course. They are no more static than we are. Our lives unfold along with them. But that first moment — considered by most astrologers to be the first intake of breath — is the door of entry into the world. The qualities of that moment govern your unique emotional, physical and mental stamp, which becomes the skeletal system that your experiences and choices in life will flesh out.

There are three major cycles used in astrology. Two of them are time cycles: the yearly succession of the seasons resulting from the Earth's orbit around the Sun, and the daily revolution of the Earth on its own axis. The third is a 'space' cycle, describing the changing angular relationships between the planets, and between the planets and the earthbound organism.

THE ZODIAC

The zodiac consists of twelve signs, which correspond with the twelve months of the year (with some slight displacement each year) as follows:

Aries	21 March–20 April
Taurus	21 April–20 May
Gemini	21 May–20 June
Cancer	21 June–22 July
Leo	23 July–22 August
Virgo	23 August–22 September
Libra	23 September–22 October
Scorpio	23 October–21 November
Sagittarius	22 November–21 December
Capricorn	22 December–19 January
Aquarius	20 January–18 February
Pisces	19 February–20 March

The dates of the Sun's entry into each sign can vary slightly each year. This means that those born on the cusp of two signs (i.e. on any of the days listed above or a day either side) will need to consult an astrologer or write to an astrological computing service to find out the exact sign in which their Sun was placed on the day they were born.

SIGN CHARACTERISTICS

A major obstacle to the acceptance of astrology is the aversion some people have to the idea that the planets and stars can influence their destiny or that the date on which they were born influences the way they act, feel and think. This resistance is of course due partly to the hocus-pocus associated with astrology and partly to the need to feel in control of our lives and characters. However, this forming of character according to our date of birth is not as arcane or arbitrary as it may seem. It is actually a natural consequence of being born at a particular point in the seasonal cycle. (This is relevant to the Northern Hemisphere seasons. A possible explanation of why these Northern Hemisphere seasonal influences apply also to those born in the Southern Hemisphere, where the seasons are opposite, is offered shortly.) In other words, the primary personality traits connected with each sign parallel its seasonal peculiarities. It is in fact possible to discover a great deal about one's personal temperament without astrology, simply by observing Nature's activities and characteristics in the month one was born. An attempt to illustrate this correspondence, with the help of references to farming and gardening guides, follows. But before we examine the signs more closely, there are some important points to note.

First, those born in the Southern Hemisphere may wonder how their personal characteristics could be derived from a seasonal influence that has nothing to do with the sign in which they were born, owing to the fact that the seasons are reversed. That is, Aries corresponds with autumn instead of spring, from which it takes its meaning, and so on throughout the zodiac.

This aspect of character classification seems to have been ignored by astrologers in the past — probably because the knowledge was not available from which to deduce an acceptable reason. However, the increased scientific interest in biological rhythms has led to the discovery of a possible explanation for this anomaly.

It was once presumed that the slump we experience in our energy levels in the early afternoon was due to the after-effects of a heavy lunch. Now, however, the origin of this phenomenon is thought to lie much deeper in our physiology: in rhythms that grew out of the habits developed by our tropical ancestors. During this hottest part of the day, the level of activity in both animals and humans naturally declined, and it is believed that this has remained intrinsic in the body's daily rhythms, no matter where we are born or live.

The same could justifiably be expected of other long-term

climatic influences. There have been many ice ages (the last ending around 10,300 years ago), and North-east Africa and the Near East, which are accepted by some archaeologists as the original Garden of Eden, or 'cradle of humanity', could conceivably have been experiencing more definite seasonal fluctuations. In other words, if we have retained daily variations in our biological cycles, it is likely that we still bear the imprint of the rhythm of the Northern Hemisphere's seasonal cycle wherever we are born, or reside, on this planet. These ideas are, of course, not conclusive and are offered merely as food for thought.

As a footnote to this, I have observed that those born in the Southern Hemisphere are not entirely without the influence of the seasonal variations of that half of the world. An Aries person, for example — who is intrinsically a spring person — will manifest certain Libran, or autumn, traits, and vice versa. This will apply to all opposite signs:

Taurus–Scorpio
Gemini–Sagittarius
Cancer–Capricorn
Leo–Aquarius
Virgo–Pisces

These traits will not be as deep-seated, however, and will therefore be less dominant.

Another type of influence on the characteristics of a sign has to do with their alternating between a 'night' (referred to as 'feminine'), and a 'day' ('masculine') association. This influence has nothing to do with gender, but represents a quality of being. For example, 'feminine' in this context refers to the receptive or magnetic qualities of energy and 'masculine' to active or electrical qualities. Both are present in each individual, to a greater or lesser extent. We all have instincts (which are in this context classed as feminine qualities), as well as intellects (or masculine qualities). The feminine/magnetic signs are Taurus, Cancer, Virgo, Scorpio, Capricorn and Pisces. The masculine/electrical signs are Aries, Gemini, Leo, Libra, Sagittarius and Aquarius.

Each sign also has a connection with one of the four elements: earth, fire, air or water. The earth signs — Taurus, Virgo and Capricorn — are connected with the material world and the senses. The air signs — Gemini, Libra and Aquarius — are concerned with mind, intellect, reason. The fire signs are passionate and inspirational and they are represented by Aries, Leo and Sagittarius, whereas the water signs — Cancer, Scorpio and Pisces — are associated with instincts and feelings.

Finally, I would like to examine one of the most common mistakes people make in assuming that the Sun sign is the only sign that influences an individual. It is vital to realise that every one of the twelve signs is present to a greater or lesser degree in each person. The signs run in a sequence and no living entity, whether plant, creature or human being, can be complete in itself — a perfect (not as in 'beautiful' but as in 'whole') manifestation of its own special type — without passing through each point in that sequence. In so doing, it absorbs the quality of each moment of the complete cycle. A tree could not be the tree we know if it were not touched by every moment of the seasonal tide which governs its growth and evolution. Nothing — and no one — lives only for one month, one sign, out of each year, retreating from existence during the rest of the cycle. That is not the way of this time-bound, linear existence of ours.

The following sign descriptions, therefore, apply to all of us inasmuch as we all have collectively, and to differing extents individually, the will to exist (Aries), the urge to take root so that something stable and enduring can be made of our lives (Taurus), the need to adapt to others and to our environment (Gemini), the domestic and nurturing instinct (Cancer), the desire to express and create (Leo), the need to contribute to society's welfare and efficiency (Virgo), the desire to relate and harmonise (Libra), the power and will to master ourselves and our environment, and to renew whatever is decaying (Scorpio), the impulse to venture into unknown realms, physical and mental, in order to become more than we are (Sagittarius), the awareness of limitations and the aspiration to overcome them and reach perfection (Capricorn), the will to find the truth, and to uplift others with it (Aquarius), and the yearning to surrender to the promise of eternal rapture made by that mysterious power that so provocatively and subtly veils the magical essence of life (Pisces). If the Sun — or any other significant point such as the Ascendant (the sign rising on the eastern horizon at the moment and place of birth), or Midheaven (that sign which is immediately overhead at birth time and place), or planet (of which there are ten) — is in one particular sign the individual concerned will be more aware of, and in touch with, the energies of that sign. This is because there is a personal channel through which the energies can flow, having been 'formed' by those patterns, so to speak.

When reading the following sign descriptions it should be remembered that each year the seasons vary. Spring does not always arrive at the end of March, nor is the harvest of every crop in all areas in the Northern Hemisphere always in September. The seasonal occurrences associated with the signs are archetypal models upon which the characteristics are based.

To those who may be concerned that the descriptions for the earlier signs are shorter than those of the later signs, it is pointed out that the forms become more differentiated the further they get from their point of origin. However, although this means that the earlier signs are less complicated, it does not follow that those born with the Sun in those signs are less complicated. There are Aries individuals who, although possibly true to their sign by being straightforward in their manner, are no less confused about life nor leading lives that are less complicated or sophisticated than the next person. And the next person may be a Piscean — a native of the twelfth sign, which is theoretically twelve times more fragmented.

In the following descriptions all quotes are taken from *The Farmer's Dictionary*, printed in the nineteenth century and edited by the Rev. John M. Wilson, and *The Gardener's Essential* by Gertrude Jekyll, 1983. These particular works were chosen because they describe the conditions and activities of each month specifically. Connections with mythological characters associated with the planets and signs are also briefly examined.

2 ASTROLOGICAL SIGNS

ARIES

FIRE (21 MARCH–20 APRIL)

Aries represents the essence of spring. At this time there is a strong sense of excited anticipation as spring rains and warmer air encourage the vibrant new life to force its way out of the dark security of its womb — the Earth — to venture out into the sunlit jeopardy of life. The Aries drive and energy derives from the same source as the instinct within the young plant to overcome any obstacle in its path to reach this single goal: to be alive. Or as Gertrude Jekyll, the famed English gardener, says of this time of the year:

> ... as yet flowers are but few; the mind is less distracted by much variety than later in the year, and is more readily concentrated on the few things that may be done ... so that the necessary restriction is a good preparation ... for the wider field of observation that is presented later.

(THE GARDENER'S ESSENTIAL)

From this sign comes the eager anticipation of experience, of release, so that the true Arian spirit never looks back. The sense of urgency arising from this instinct produces the human qualities of courage and daring on the one hand while on the other it also brings impatience and impulsiveness. Similarly, the Arian spirit of competitiveness is the same as that push within the green shoots to compete with each other for a place in the light and warmth of the sun.

In mythology, fiery Aries is Ares, or Mars, the God of War, the planet designated as ruler of Aries. This connection also correlates with the Aries need to conquer. However, a strong Aries influence in a horoscope might detract from the follow-through necessary to complete a project once the challenge has been met and the early obstacles conquered.

The Arian desire to lead and will to win exist in all walks of life. Any area where the pioneering spirit of adventure and challenge is needed, where there are new territories to discover, people to lead or conquer, or obstacles to break through, are all well-suited to the Arian temperament. This vigour is necessary in the fields of sport, sales, industry and physical labour — in all those who revel in physical exertion. Additionally, Mars' rulership of iron and steel gives us through Aries (and also Scorpio to some extent, because it is co-ruled by Mars) those who use or build machinery, motor mechanics, engineers, iron and steelworkers.

Aries is the life force; it is the vital spark that drives all living things towards the light. Without this quality no human being would ever come into existence, let alone live out a life span.

TAURUS

EARTH (21 APRIL–20 MAY)

Taurus is the second phase of spring, when Nature is still new, still tender and unfledged. The Taurean is essentially aware of this vulnerability. Consequently, where Aries strains upward and outward, Taurus digs down.

The energy used in the Arian battle to emerge into conscious life is in Taurus channelled instead into the act of establishing the new existence. The urge now is to secure the position, to develop a root system that will give stability and ensure permanent sustenance, therefore ensuring the future.

In the human sphere, the Taurean achieves this by acquiring material assets, by building resources. Taurus needs to possess — to have — in order to feel secure. The Taurean's sense of identity in fact emerges during the course of discovering how to manage and use these possessions and resources. This is why an emphasis on Taurus in a horoscope will often produce a manager, accountant, banker and financier.

On the surface of it, it is difficult to equate money with Nature. Yet the patterns of life emerge in their proper places regardless of whether or not the human mind understands the connection. In this respect it was a delight to find in an old and out-of-print copy of *The Farmer's Dictionary* the recommendation that: 'the balancing of the yearly accounts of the farm is done with most convenience and suitableness in May'.

Taurus is ruled by two planets: the Earth, associating the sign with agriculture and horticulture, and Venus — Goddess of Beauty, Art and Music — which contributes to the creation of singers, composers and other musicians and artists. In May:

. . . the lark sings and the cuckoo is often and loudly heard . . .

The face of every landscape daily improves throughout May, in interest and beauty. The fields, the woods, the orchards, the gardens, daily increase their attractions and afford incentives to gratitude and admiration.
(THE FARMER'S DICTIONARY)

The song of the nightingale and the ring of the woodman's axe gain a rich musical quality . . . (THE GARDENER'S ESSENTIAL)

Like the poetic concept of the Earth being fertilised by a comet — that adventurous traveller from foreign regions — Aries is the fiery spirit, which Taurus, matter, embodies. And, as *The Farmer's Dictionary* says, May is the time that 'Breeding mares should receive the male in order that they may foal in April'. (All other earth signs immediately follow fire signs also.) Taurus rules the physical form and its senses, which are an avenue for the experience and development of the human spirit, as well as the body.

Taurus is the need in human nature for indestructibility and a sense of continuity. It is the same force that drives a human being to build his or her life on a base of enduring values and qualities. Without this urge we would not have had any continuity of human civilisation. That is the Taurean task.

GEMINI

AIR (21 MAY–20 JUNE)

Toward the end of [May] the air has a freshness, a softness and a fragrance which exhilarate the spirits and improve the health; and animated nature displays a multitudinous, a sprightliness, an unceasing activity, and a joyous gladness which evoke and sustain the most pleasurable emotions.   (THE FARMER'S DICTIONARY)

And Gertrude Jekyll is in complete agreement on this.

June — the time of perfect young summer, the fulfilment of the promise of the earlier months, and with as yet no sign to remind one that its fresh young beauty will ever fade ... And now, in the morning how good it is to see the brilliant light of the blessed summer day ... and to feel one's own thankfulness of heart, and that it is good to live ...   (THE GARDENER'S ESSENTIAL)

Gemini represents the final phase of spring. The cycle of growth, which commenced in Aries and was established in Taurus, can now safely and joyfully proliferate in Gemini, so nature fills the world with a kaleidoscopic profusion of flora and fauna. The Gemini being is filled with this sense of teeming possibilities and dashes back and forth in a constant state of discovery. Being an air sign, the attraction is a mental one. It is the information and ideas surrounding Gemini people that fascinate them so. And they gather up all this information and file it away — just in case it's needed in the future. It is Gemini's rampant appetite for data and facts that creates in humanity a curiosity about the tremendous diversity to be found in life.

Geminis can be so busy discovering, however, that they forget to look for a meaning behind all that surface data they are so eagerly collecting, and this can cause them to spread themselves too thinly. Nonetheless, Gemini's primary function *is* to spread themselves around, to give the rest of us a taste of the joys of spring.

This sign is linked with the lungs, which take in oxygen

to vitalise the body and then release the transformed oxygen back into the environment in a form not only useable by other species but also necessary to their continued existence. The exchange of air between the lungs and the environment parallels the vital exchange of ideas between Gemini and the rest of the world — which is why their life food is interaction with others. This is, incidentally, a fundamental need for all human beings.

Gemini is ruled by the planet Mercury: Messenger of the Gods; the agent, go-between, gatherer and disseminator of news and information. It is responsible for the mind's capacity to make connections between all the separate pieces of information. Consequently, it governs the nervous system in the body, which in society corresponds with the telephone, telegraph, postal and transport systems.

The desire to cover such a wide variety of possibilities makes Gemini very changeable — a quality not usually considered a virtue. However, this quality in another form is Gemini's most important attribute, for it is in the Gemini phase of development that living organisms learn how to *adapt* to their environment, this being a fundamental necessity for the survival of all living creatures.

CANCER

WATER (21 JUNE–22 JULY)

The first day of Cancer is the longest day of the year in the Northern Hemisphere: it is the Summer Solstice. As the month proceeds, the Sun grows hotter, and

> ... *the greater part of animated nature sinks into lassitude, retreats into shelter, or drops into repose; birds languish and secrete themselves in the woods; sheep court the shade and coolness of lofty enclosures; horses crowd beneath the shade of umbrageous trees; cows stand ruminating in the cool pond; swine revel in the mire* ...
>
> (THE FARMER'S DICTIONARY)

At this time of the year, in order for plants and animals to attain maturity, they need to be nurtured and protected.

> *... any reasonable number of beasts may, during every day of the month, receive abundance of food in the yard or stall ... high fed ones are apt to break bounds, [so] the fences ought to be maintained in perfectly good condition. All sheep, during July, ought to have access to shade and pure water, and ewes ... ought to be well kept in order that they may be in a healthy and strong state for the ram in August.*
>
> (THE FARMER'S DICTIONARY)

Coincidently, the instinct in human nature to protect and care for its young develops out of this Cancerian phase in the cycle of the seasons.

Fruits that are forming now produce a thick skin or shell to prevent damage to their tender contents. Similarly, Cancerians build walls around those under their aegis, as well as around themselves, in defence of their own sensitive interior: their feelings.

These inclinations are reinforced by another more subtle pressure, for the turning point in the cyclic pulsation of growth and decay has been reached. Although there is no immediately visible evidence of this, daily now the darkness is steadily increasing. Cancerians are ruled by the ever-changing Moon, from which they acquire their susceptibility to the subtle tidal pulls and undercurrents of life, along with a reputation for psychic ability. An awareness of these obscure but irresistible changes seeps into the deeper levels of the Cancerian psyche, pushing them to create a safe haven to retreat to should they feel threatened. This is why they are frequently so attached to their homes and families.

Cancer's function is to support, give succour, sanctuary, sympathy, solace and comfort. Therefore, it rules all domestic and homemaking matters, hotels, restaurants, caretaking, the supply of commodities for a comfortable and smooth-running home life, and some aspects of building and real estate.

In astrology, the Moon is traditionally regarded as representative of the Soul. It is the great archetypal Mother: feminine counterpart of the Sun, Spirit and Father. Cancer rules the womb and physical sustenance. But, being a water sign, it also relates to emotional sustenance, which is just as vital to our well-being and equilibrium. To fulfil these needs, it gives us mothers (of both sexes) to enfold us with tender care and devotion to ensure that we will survive infancy and grow to adulthood.

LEO

FIRE (23 JULY–22 AUGUST)

> *The transformations of most insects and of some other animals are now completed . . . the frog has emerged from the tadpole and leaves its watery home to enjoy its gymnastics on land; and the living inmates of many kinds of eggs, from the microscopic to the great in size, have burst from their imprisonment, and luxuriate in the energies and feats of life . . .* (THE FARMER'S DICTIONARY)

In deep summer, Nature celebrates this liberation in a pageant of floral and elemental ostentation: the drama of a thunderstorm, ravaging her own creations; the flash of lightning and the crack of thunder, which humans have so often equated with the wrath of the gods.

Here indeed is the voice of ultimate authority and both Leo and its ruling body, the Sun, are the Father and the Creator: the fire and brimstone God of the Old Testament, whose command his subjects ignored at their peril.

The Sun is now coalescing with the power of elemental nature and is imbued with the capacity to destroy life as well as to bestow it. Fiery Leo — the sign in which the Sun is at its most potent — exults in this sense of dominion. But after the smouldering tension of heat and dust and swelter has been released in this grand theatrical crescendo, the wearied senses are excited anew. The rains have rejuvenated flower, leaf and grass, intensifying the vibrancy of colour, and the freshly washed air is sharp with the fragrance of revivified Nature.

Leo is constrained to express this 'divine creation'; this life, or spirit. However, it is difficult for Leo to avoid identifying with the power source because it is to him so clearly within himself. This belief lures the ego into the delusion that what is produced is solely its own doing. However, the tadpole does not create the frog. Neither does the father consciously create the child, even though he provides the means for this creation to occur. All is accomplished by a force that is greater than he is. And of all the star signs, Leo can be the least capable of the kind of humility that truly admits to the existence of a force greater than himself. He may be able to admit intellectually to the concept but to do so with his whole being would mean being swamped by elemental nature; by the power of the collective. And this would threaten his very reason for being, for it is Leo's destiny, his zodiacal task, to search for, find and set free the as yet nascent individuality which has been forming since Aries.

Leo is the instrument through which this creative thrust manifests itself, coloured highly by his unique qualities and style. Consequently, whether the final product is a child of his flesh, of his spirit, or of his very self, to Leo it is an extension of his identity and it must bear his stamp for the same reason it was said that 'God made this world in order to see Himself', or as one of India's great spiritual leaders, Sri Aurobindo, said in his monumental epic poem, *Savitri:*

> The Spirit shall look out
> through Matter's gaze
> And Matter shall reveal
> the Spirit's face.

Leo's effort to make a dramatic impact on his environment is directly attributable to this need to see his self reflected back to him — if not in his creative product itself, at least in the recognition by others of its significance. If possible, he hopes such recognition will take the form of reverence, such as we would give to the glory of a summer sunset or the awe and respect we would accord a raging storm, or a scorching desert waste.

Leo rules the heart. The heart is as much the centre of our bodies at a physical level, of our emotions at a psychological level, or of our will at a mental level, as the Sun is the centre of our lives and of our solar system. Naturally, Leo feels he too is the centre of his universe. This sign's instinct is to shine, to give light, warmth and love, to enliven, to play. Leo is the child as well as the father, the beloved as well as the lover, the creation as well as the creator. This is what he feels whether he realises it or not, and whether or not he is able to articulate these instincts.

Should Leo find himself in an unsympathetic environment: among people who ignore him, or where he cannot give vent to his creative powers in a way that will enthuse and enliven others, then he himself will shrivel and lose that wonderful magnanimity, innocence and ingenuousness that are his trademarks and a light to us all, for he has lost his point of reference. He has lost his contact with his source. Should this happen, these superlative qualities become perverted by the thwarted ego into the traits for which Leo is notorious: egocentricity, boastfulness, childishness, temper tantrums and arrogance.

The compulsion Leo has to express his creative force makes all the world a stage. From this sign come many who are connected with the theatre — from actors, dramatists and producers to the patrons who appreciate and support them (and who fulfil this expressive urge vicariously).

Leo's connection with the child within, along with this sign's 'luxuriation in the energies and feats of life' connects it with the fields of sport and gymnastics. This same link, coupled with Leo's need to be a guiding force, elicits our innate desire to educate our children, thereby making it one of the signs that gives us teachers.

Out of Leo's compulsion to give form to the creative urge comes the inspiration to reproduce and interpret art, poetry, literature and music.

As with all the signs, all of this is relevant not only to the Leo individual. We each have a spirit, a heart, a child within.

We each have the urge to express, create, re-create, procreate, or fulfil, in whatever way we are able, the magical essence of life, and of the human spirit.

Incidentally, it is interesting to note that, from the Earth's point of view, the Sun (representing the male principle), and the Moon (the female principle) appear equal in size. The Sun's apparent diameter varies between 32'55'' and 31'31'' of arc (depending on the Earth's slightly varying distance from the Sun); while that of the Moon ranges from 33'31'' to 29'22'' (which is similarly governed by the Moon's distance at any time from the Earth). This means that despite the enormous disparity in their actual dimensions, their distances from the Earth are precisely proportioned to accommodate this symbolic equality between the two primary powers of light.

VIRGO

EARTH (23 AUGUST–22 SEPTEMBER)

Here, at the end of summer, it is time to concentrate on the everyday business of living. Preparation must be made for harvesting — as suggested by the sheaves depicted in the emblem for Virgo. The creative productivity of Leo has now to be gathered and classified. Plants have to be divided and replanted so that roots can be established before the frosts and cold winds arrive. It is a time of the year when efficiency, order and industry are vital to future survival.

> *A farmer's cares, in reference to harvest . . . are many and grave and almost oppressive. A large portion of his temporal interests are at stake; various methods must be practised with different crops; many minds must be controlled; multitudes of labours must be commanded and inspected; hundreds of minute and concurrent provisions, in regard to both the work-people and their work, must be made; . . . all the contingencies of weather must be studied . . . all the favourable influences of it strenuously followed, and all the malign effects of it conjectured and combated . . . the farmer has daily and nightly . . .*

much need of skill, energy, vigilance, and continual self-possession ...
Yet [he] so fully anticipates the work of harvest, so thoroughly prepares
for it ... that he ... promptly accommodates himself, though it were
hundreds of times over, to changes of tact and prospect.

(THE FARMER'S DICTIONARY)

These are all typical Virgo characteristics, out of which arise the human powers to differentiate and to discriminate. The biological correspondence to this is 'natural selection', which allows for variation within species. This in turn contributes to survival, for selection is closely related to adaptation, which is the function of Gemini who is Virgo's Mercurial partner. Selection also leads to constant refinement, such as in plant propagation, which must be carried out at this time. The healthiest and best plants are chosen, not only to ensure survival but also to improve quality.

The constant need to analyse and correctly categorise is synonymous with Virgo. Unfortunately, because many of us are not nearly so worried about such a perfect order, the Virgoan is constantly confronted by our muddle and confusion and by the imperfections that result from careless ways. This is all anathema to Virgo and results in her penchant for finding fault and criticising.

Although Virgo is an Earth sign and so many of her skills lie in dealing with the material world, she is ruled by the 'mental' planet, Mercury. This combination compels her to dissect, grade and systematise every bit of the universe — if at all possible — making science a natural product of the Virgo phase of development. This again complements Mercury's other sign, Gemini, which is the fact-gatherer.

Virgo's famed efficiency and methodical organisation makes office work a frequently occupied field which satiates the Virgo hunger for order and neatness.

This sign is also connected with care and nourishment, but along the lines of dutiful supply and maintenance, in contrast with the Cancerian function of instinctive nurturing and protectiveness.

Virgo's concern with the supply of food for the maintenance of the organism creates an interest in health and diet. In these matters Virgoans can become faddish and fastidious (as they may also become in other matters). This is due partly at least to their proneness to allergies. Also, Virgo being the zodiac's primary candidate for the worry olympics, mental hyperactivity can increase their need for nutrients as well as diminish their capacity to absorb them, particularly those that feed the nervous system. Virgoans' continual fretting, which can make them fussy and pedantic, coupled with their preoccupation with bodily well-being, makes them frequently hypochondriacal.

The emblem associated with Mercury is the caduceus, which has been allied with healing since at least 2600 B.C. The symbol of two intertwined serpents, such as appear encircling the staff, was thought to embody equilibrium, wholeness and, therefore, health. The caduceus is, of course, the symbol adopted by the medical profession and in consonance with this, Virgo also produces doctors and other healers.

Owing to its association with the small intestine, Virgo is particularly connected with natural ingested substances that cure. Virgo's opposite sign, Pisces, has rulership over drugs, so this polarity of Virgo/Pisces brings into the Virgo domain conventional medicines as well as 'alternative' ones.

The Virgo concern with the supply of everyday necessities leads them into the clothing industry where they excel in both design and production. The former talent stems from an inherent sense of balance (back to the caduceus symbolism), which gives a skill in putting things together in their proper place — matching and balancing colours and accessories, as well as lines. (This field of work also gives this fastidious sign an opportunity to tidy up the people who occupy her world.) Their production skills arise from the need to coordinate the many operations that lead to the finished garment, so that all stages mesh together smoothly like the proverbial well-oiled machine.

At a biological level, this same urge promotes the ease with which the workings of the various bodily systems are integrated. At a social level, it enhances the integration of each individual into the working community.

LIBRA

AIR (23 SEPTEMBER–22 OCTOBER)

The first degree of Libra corresponds with the Autumnal Equinox. Therefore, this sign falls exactly opposite the first zodiacal sign, Aries: an opposition that is crucially significant because it is symbolic of all the dualities of life, right down to the electrical and magnetic energies underlying our existence. In Libra, an equilibrium is attained and there is a pause as a conscious adjustment is made towards the now obviously encroaching darkness. Up to now this has only been experienced at a subconscious level by those signs following the Summer Solstice — Cancer, Leo and Virgo. In Libra, the confrontation of the personal with the impersonal, of the individual with society, of self with other, is out in the open.

As the Libran sense of well-being depends on balance and harmony, such continual confrontations make of him a strategist and connects the sign with war, as well as with peace. (Winston Churchill and Adolf Hitler had Libra rising.) The task set for Libra at this phase of development in the zodiac is to relate consciously and purposely to those opposing factions — that is, to society, the greater whole.

As Libra represents the first social step a human being takes, these individuals prefer on the whole to meet the rest of the world one at a time. This is why Libra is the sign of relationships *per se*.

Many astrologers connect Libra with the as yet to be located 'planet' Proserpine (Persephone) (thought to exist beyond the orbit of Pluto, owing to the perturbations in that planet's path which have not as yet been accounted for satisfactorily by any other phenomena).

In mythology, Proserpine spent half the year in the Underworld with Pluto (Hades), who kidnapped her and took her as his wife. The other half of the year she lived above ground with her doting mother, Ceres (Demeter), Goddess of the Harvest. (Note that in the month of October hibernation is not yet in full swing although it has begun.) Ceres, the asteroid, is considered one of the rulers of the sign of Virgo; Pluto rules Scorpio. The sign sequence is Virgo, Libra, Scorpio. As Proserpine swings back and forth between two worlds, so Nature reflects this myth in October:

Much of the work proper to September may, by the backwardness of a season, or the prevalence of unfavourable harvest weather, be prolonged into October; and a considerable portion of the work proper to October frequently requires to be postponed till November.

(THE FARMER'S DICTIONARY)

All this seesawing and discord makes Libra nervy, even physically ill, unless he can withdraw periodically and regain his poise. This is why Libra spends so much time trying to restore accord between himself and others, and also amongst others — which is what makes him such a potentially good tactitian and diplomat. His most pressing question, however, and one that rarely leaves him, is: which one is right?

In the many versions of the myth, we never hear what Proserpine thinks about it all, for she is mute. Nonetheless, presumably she loves her mother, and she is committed to her husband, but the two live on different planes of existence and can never be reconciled. Proserpine is a passive pawn in their game, forever condemned by her loyalties or her fate to alternate between these eternal enemies: the force that nurtures life and the one that takes it away (although both forces have other aspects that make them, in the end, equally desirable and loathsome).

Proserpine may or may not have feelings about all this, but Libra does. Libra feels responsible and tries to please and placate both sides. His greatest bane is that he identifies so readily with both sides that he understands how both are right from their own viewpoints. Being forced to choose between two or more alternatives, however minor they may be, can almost paralyse Libra because he feels that the choices he makes will have momentous effects on his future well-being. This is especially so where human welfare hinges on a sudden turn in the weather:

> *October weather, when understood with practical reference to the*
> *condition and operations of the farm, is the period of comparative or*
> *tolerable mildness which immediately precedes such an inclement*
> *transition to rain, snow, or frost, as puts an arrest upon most of the*
> *labours of the field.* (THE FARMER'S DICTIONARY)

The future depends on the right choices being made now: when to plough, when to sow fresh seed?

Libra's constant comparisons and concern for rightness and fairness give rise to the human concept of justice. This is the only zodiacal sign that does not have a living creature — human or animal — as its emblem. Instead it has an impersonal object: a set of scales — the Scales of Justice. This suggests that at their best Libran evaluations can be objective and impartial, which makes Libra a fair lawyer (assuming he can reach a decision). The sign also produces good counsellors — in whatever field is personally favoured.

The difficulty experienced in taking a stand can open up the field of politics to some Librans. The problem here is that Libra wants to do the right thing by everyone, as well as to be liked by everyone at the same time.

Libra's main preoccupation, however, is with relationships. Libra is very much aware of 'something missing'; as if he were occupying only one side of the scales. This impels him to seek company so that he has someone against whom he can react, or who reacts against him, so he can check that his values, ideas, likes and dislikes are really valid. (Dark only exists because light exists against which to measure its relativity.) But although Librans can be very strongly attracted to their partners, the impersonality of the sign's underlying nature can cause them to see the partner as an object at times, rather than as a human being. Even the influence of the Goddess of Love, Venus, who rules this sign as well as the sign of Taurus, is affected by this impersonal quality, which can make a fickle lover of Libra. (As ruler of Taurus, Venus is steadied by that sign's fixed, earthy nature.)

Coincident with the Libran awareness of differences, the

month of October is a time of vivid contrast. Nature now breaks out her warmest and most brilliant hues — perhaps in reaction to the coming austerities. The blazing crimsons and oranges and the delicate yellows, splashed here and there with bright emerald green moss and occasionally frosted white, are gorgeously set off against the particularly sharp blue of autumn skies.

This phase of evolution, along with the Venusian influence, brings out other facets and skills in people, such as in beautification by decoration, of both human beings and their environment. As with Virgo, there is a harmonious sense of proportion and line, and especially of colour, which is so strongly connected with Libra. This gives Librans an innate concept of 'ideal form', which encompasses many levels, from social to physical, and it is manifested in artistic, musical and cultural activities.

But not least of all, the powerful social awareness of this sign gives to humanity the skills with which a society can be built and can function successfully, for ultimately Libra gives us the need, desire and capacity to relate to each other.

SCORPIO

WATER (23 OCTOBER–21 NOVEMBER)

November has the reputation of being ... dark, unsettled, and stormy, and frequently wrapped in fogs and snows ... The flowers are gone; the long grass stands ... withered, bleached, and sere; the fern is red and shrivelled ... the plants which waved their broad white umbels to the summer breeze, now, like skeleton trophies of death, rattle their dry and hollow branches to the autumnal winds ... The migratory birds ... are no longer to be seen, and their successors are ... less mirthful and more shy and seclusive; the frog sinks to the bottom of ponds and ditches and buries itself in the mud; (other creatures) creep into holes in the earth and into similar other retreats, there to lie torpid till spring; ... and bats retire into old barns, caves, and deserted buildings.

(THE FARMER'S DICTIONARY)

♏ Here we have reached the point in our yearly cycle where the growing darkness can no longer be kept at bay with tricks and trappings and other distractions. Our dark primeval mother is inexorably drawing the life forces back into herself, to renew them.

Relationships, both personal, and the individual's relationship to the group, are still the main arena for this ongoing play of Nature. In Scorpio, Libra's need for reciprocation swells to a passion to fuse the two opposing principles ('me' and 'you') into a single whole — on all levels: physical, mental, emotional, social (i.e. love relationships, business partnerships, group relationships).

On an abstract level this passion is present in the type of scientist or occultist who seeks primary causes or unifying theories. Anyone with an emphasis on Scorpio or its ruling planet, Pluto, has to deal with the same urge that is so strong in Nature at this time of the year: the urge to overpower, to possess, and also to be possessed. The problem of just how much of oneself one should give and how much to take pertains to us all. However, for Scorpio there is inevitably a tendency to overdo it. At the same time she resists this pull because to effect such a total union the identity or personal ego must be surrendered, must 'die', if only for a moment, so that something greater can come into being.

There are many occasions in our lives when we have to give up and let go, whether of some person or a particular way of life. The sexual act, giving birth, and finally death itself, are all forms of surrender. In fact, all change entails a death of something, so that a new phase of development can begin.

All of life is perpetually faced with this threat of extinction, of being sucked back into the dark womb of Nature. But the drive to exist gives us the fire and will to resist. At this time of the year, even though this power is dormant and withdrawn, it is no weaker. It is in fact more concentrated and hangs on grimly — to survive, to reproduce, to begin again, revitalised and renewed.

Scorpio's reserve, inhibition and secretiveness are due to her need for a time to herself in order to understand and integrate the mysterious turmoil she is feeling within. This withdrawal can lead to misunderstanding, for when winter begins her long siege and all energies are focused on preparation for survival, there is no time to explain. Nor is there room for embellishment.

All fattening ... sheep ought to receive as much as they can possibly eat, yet without ... waste ... squirrels, rats, and field-mice shut themselves up with their winter stores ... The borders of the fields should be thoroughly cleaned from ... rubbishy ... vegetation ... water-furrows which contain stagnant water should be cleansed ... the carting home of sufficient supplies of fuel ought to be attended to.

(THE FARMER'S DICTIONARY)

Waste and 'frivolous ornamentation' tend to draw out the Scorpio sting and if tolerance is not developed can eventually lead to cynicism.

The Scorpio instinct for the ruthless elimination of all that does not advance the cause is most evident in the spheres of corporate business, politics and war. Here there are no — what Scorpio perceives to be — 'extraneous' scruples or morals disguising Nature's raw and savage anarchy. The same qualities are present (in diluted form) in the triumphant satisfaction with which a housewife on a cleaning rampage empties cupboards and drawers, cellars and attics, of all she deems obsolete, outworn or unable to be transformed and recycled — usually much to the discomfort of the rest of the household.

Scorpio's strengths are her resourcefulness, her power for regeneration, organisation, management and control. She is the manipulating force in politics and business, forever battling against the odds. In terms of power, money, or both, she often accrues as much as she can in order to defend herself, and those to whom she feels bound, from want or obliteration should winter (or the tax man) prove too severe.

The ongoing battle deep within the psyche between the

primal forces of survival and surrender builds up a tremendous tension, which may eventually erupt volcanically.

Scorpio is a water sign, yet being ruled by Pluto, God of the Underworld, and Mars, fiery God of War, it is more like liquid fire. The feelings run deep and strong. And the intensity of her frustration, rage, jealousy, passion and grief, erupting from her very core, reshape her whole nature, like the molten lava that bursts forth from the Earth's heart and changes the face of the land. Harnessed and directed, these are the forces that enable us to accomplish our goals, regardless of obstructions. However, as these forces are rarely selective, they can often function to the detriment of the body or mind of whoever is trying to fulfil their commands. Often, they become focused on a particular objective or individual, and become obsessive. Unchannelled and unexpressed, these compulsions are destructive.

It is understandable that Scorpio has come to be viewed with the same suspicion and fear with which we think of the creature that is its namesake. Yet Scorpio has another symbol: the Eagle. For there are two sides to her powers, both of which are necessary to life.

As destroyer, she enables us to tear down and eliminate all decaying or obsolete forms. As restorer she transforms and rebuilds these into new, more relevant forms. At a mundane level, this part of the cycle is expressed by those who renovate the old and broken-down — a building, a piece of furniture, a car or business. It also refers to those who work in the fields of healing: the acupuncturist, masseur, psychic healer, or the surgeon and psychologist who cut deep into the body and psyche respectively to eliminate the root cause of a problem.

The Scorpio urge to withdraw deep into herself to re-contact her power source is manifested in an urge to penetrate the surface of all things and gives rise to an interest in research, archaeology and mining. But it also associates this sign with death, black magic and other necromantic and sorcerous phenomena, or anything else that makes us uncomfortable, guilty, afraid or disgusted.

Yet, without this Scorpio phase, we would not willingly

relinquish our outworn psychological and physical structures, our old truths for new. We would escape, at great cost, the fires of psychological torment which each renewed contact with our volcanic origins incurs. For these are the fires that burn away each layer of the social and egoistic cocoon which encases the essential self, so that the fabled phoenix — symbol of the victory of light over darkness — can rise anew out of its own ashes.

SAGITTARIUS

FIRE (22 NOVEMBER–21 DECEMBER)

In Sagittarius, the night force has her greatest dominion, for at the first degree of Capricorn (which follows), it is the Winter Solstice, and the light again begins to grow. This is truly the darkest hour before the dawn.

> *December is sometimes designated the gloomiest month in the year ...*
> *In some years, it has prevailingly a dry bracing frost; in others, it has*
> *an almost uninterrupted series of fogs, and drizzling rains; in others, it*
> *maintains a ... proportion of the clearness and mildness which*
> *characterize a remarkably fine autumn; in many, it acquires ... a*
> *stern, relentless, wintry character; and in most ... it possesses a*
> *combination of wetness, storminess, and comparative mildness ... the*
> *vast majority of ... plants are in a state of profound repose, resting*
> *their roots dormantly beneath the soil ...*
>
> (THE FARMER'S DICTIONARY)

While the life force continues to retreat, or at least at this time is quiescent, Sagittarius strains fervently outward and away from the subterranean chaos of Scorpio, and the confines of his earthbound nature, towards higher, more lofty realms. In the Sagittarian glyph, this effort is symbolised by the arrow, which is also a phallic symbol. Here, already, is the Sagittarian dilemma, for he is bound by the limitations of the same energy that gives him the impetus to escape his bondage. He is deterred from grappling with his own instincts, which are spontaneous, irrepressible and inseparable from his will to live, so he grapples instead with collective instincts. These in turn reflect back on him and bind him from the outside, for this is the phase in which society's rules are developed — not 'justice' which belongs to Libra, but simply 'law'.

Like Jupiter, the Roman God of Gods and ruling planet of this sign, Sagittarius yearns to roam free in the garden of sensual delight. Jupiter was constantly brought smartly back into line by his wife, Juno, whose righteous indignation and revenge unceasingly dogged his infidelities. Similarly, the social conscience of Sagittarius, often also in the form of a wife, or else his own regard for religious or social morality, puts restraints on his amorous spirit. However, although the night force binds it, the fiery essence of life is bursting to break out of its wintry grave to find and sample the warmth and the young flush of spring that the coming Solstice heralds. And with this end in mind, preparations are made. In the words of Gertrude Jekyll:

> Now we go into the copse and cut the trees that have been provisionally marked ... The best of the birch tops are cut into pea-sticks, a clever slanting cut with the hand-bill leaving them pointed and ready for use ... we get good straight stakes for Dhalias and Hollyhocks, also bean-poles; while the rather straight-branched boughs are cut into branching sticks for Michaelmas Daisies, and special lengths are got ready for various kinds of plants. To provide all this in winter, when other work is slack or impossible, is an important matter ... for all gardeners know how distressing and harassing it is to find themselves without the right sort of sticks or stakes in summer ... no precious time is lost, and a tidy withe-bound bundle of the right sort is always at hand.
>
> (THE GARDENER'S ESSENTIAL)

Such is the Sagittarian foresight, for which this sign is renowned. The stick, or staff, is a symbol of support, as well as being a weapon. (In the suit of Wands in the Tarot — clubs in modern card decks — the wands are shown sprouting green leaves. This is the Sagittarian symbol of his faith and hope in ever-renewed life.) Similarly, Sagittarius gains a sense of support, and of confidence and faith in the future, from his personal beliefs because they reflect those of his society or other group with which he identifies. But although supportive, his faith — like the stake — can become a crutch, a piece of dead wood like the rigid dogmas and belief systems of a religion that has only its ceremonies and words left because it has lost its essence.

The determination of one religious faith to convert another, and our need to convince others to believe what we believe so that we may continue to believe, also arises out of the Sagittarian phase and is the dark face of human faith.

If his convictions are shattered, Sagittarius goes into temporary shock because doubt is thrown on the architect who designed them, which to Sagittarius could be either society or God. As a result, his support system disintegrates and he is like a lost soul until he can find something with which to replace it, which he will then uphold with equal verve and commitment.

Usually, Sagittarius refuses to be daunted or to go under, which the previous sign, Scorpio, can eventually do with such abandon that it almost seems as if she enjoys it. But when Sagittarius is flailing around in the mire of despair, no one would accuse him of enjoying it. He is so utterly abject, so hurt. His faith, which, like all the fire signs, can give him a childlike innocence, is shaken because he cannot comprehend that fate could deal him such a cruel blow. Perhaps, too, it is the dramatic contrast with his usual jubilance that makes it seem such a drastic change.

This period of the year is the 'season of goodwill' and there is no doubt that this sign is funadmentally of goodwill, for he is a social creature, generous and sympathetic. Quoting the Rev. John M. Wilson again:

During December, almost all insects (and creatures) which have escaped destruction are inert in their winter-torpor ... Yet such ... as retain the exercise of their instincts, perception, and locomotivity, become more confiding in man, and excite much more tender feelings of interest than

during summer or autumn; and various agreeable families of the
feathered tribe ... arrive upon our shores, and ... challenge the
attention, and interest the feelings, during the snows of December."

(THE FARMER'S DICTIONARY)

Another rulership assigned to Sagittarius is the planetoid
Chiron, which orbits between Saturn and Uranus. The mythological centaur, Chiron, was struck in the leg by a poisonous
arrow. It inflicted such a terrible wound it could not be healed.
Because Chiron was immortal he was doomed to live in perpetual
agony. Sagittarius rules the hips and thighs, including the sciatic
nerve, and many astrologers report a history of temporary
or permanent limps among those in whose charts this sign
is strongly emphasised.

Thus, the fiery Archer may aim for the stars but his feet
are firmly rooted in the earth so that he can touch those ideals
only with his 'arrows': his mind or spirit. (For those who
may be wondering, Chiron was later released from his torment
when he gave up his immortality to save the life of another,
with true Sagittarian altruism.)

This restraint means that for Sagittarius everything must
contribute towards the reaching of a goal, whether it be a
personal, social or spiritual goal. Or else it must contribute
in some way to the ideological support that the doctrines and
systems of the group can give to an individual.

Where Sagittarius's opposite sign, Gemini, asks 'what is
life?', Sagittarius asks 'what is the meaning of life?'. This,
coupled with the association with Chiron, a wise teacher and
healer, confers upon the often childlike Sagittarian a worldly
wisdom and kindness, albeit of a rough type. These traits in
Sagittarius give rise to philosophers, theosophists, theologists,
sociologists, as well as teachers and theorists.

His wide-ranging spirit, which is appalled by restriction of
any kind, and which sets his sights on distant shores (both
physical and mental), makes some Sagittarians world travellers,
travel guides and agents, pilots, stewards, linguists, astronomers,
astronauts, sportsmen and import/exporters.

Because of his social and ethical conscience, Sagittarius can be a puritan or a moralist, whose conviction in 'the law' leads him into the courtroom, the pulpit, or onto the soapbox, to give vent to his righteous indignation. The same conviction, coupled with a readiness to take enthusiastic and swift advantage of any opportunity, also makes Sagittarius a top salesman, businessman, entrepreneur, and leads him into advertising, journalism and publishing.

Sagittarius is both Jupiter and Juno: both the will to soar beyond the confines of the body, Earth and its mundane demands, as well as the force that nails his feet to the ground. He is the law — and the society that made it and must live by it — the prosecutor, and the defendant. He is the happy-go-lucky spirit of opportunism and hedonism, the sinner as well as the saint. He is the satyr and the god.

Sagittarius provides the pattern for a society that supports and protects the individuals who comprise it and also gives each one the opportunity to advance and grow.

He looks to the future and aims his arrow of hope, guided on its way by his irrepressible spirit of good-natured optimism, to the new life that will rise again in the spring.

CAPRICORN

EARTH (22 DECEMBER–19 JANUARY)

How endlessly beautiful is woodland in winter! Today there is a thin mist; just enough to make a background of tender blue mystery ... and to show any defect in the grouping of near trees. No day could be better for deciding which trees are to come down; there is not too much at a time within sight; just one good picturefull and no more.

Now the splendid richness of the common holly is more than ever impressive, with its solid masses of full, deep colour, and its wholesome look of perfect health and vigour. Sombrely cheerful ... sombre by reason of the extreme depth of tone, and yet cheerful from the look of

glad life, and from the assurance of warm shelter and protecting comfort
to bird and beast and neighbouring vegetation. The picture is made
complete by the slender shafts of the silver-barked birches . . . Has any
tree so graceful a way of throwing up its stems as the birch? . . . [in a]
never-failing rightness of free-swinging poise and perfect balance. The
. . . bark is here silvery-white and there milk-white [with] the faintest
tinge of rosy flush . . . the stem is clouded and banded with delicate
grey, and with the silver-green of lichen. [In young trees] the bark is
dark in colour, and lies in thick and extremely rugged upright ridges.

(THE GARDENER'S ESSENTIAL)

These are the colours and the moods of Capricorn:
subdued, stately, classic, assured.

In this sign we reach the darkest day — the Winter
Solstice. But at its moment of greatest triumph, the balance
of power is reversed. From here on, the days lengthen,
imperceptibly at first, as the ascending light force gains strength
once more. But for now it must patiently bide its time.

At this time of the year, which is mostly frosty or snow-
bound, the growth of plants and the movement of creatures
(and people) are restricted. This disciplinary quality of January
is the trademark of Capricorn, whose task is, in part, to curtail
impatience in order to prevent the premature expansion that
could mean injury, or even extinction, to an organism at this
time. Therefore, the Capricorn influence works to slow down
the progress of any project, skill, ambition, relationship —
or any other type of situation — should an attempt be made
to reap the fruits before they have properly ripened. Capricorn
is also the brick wall, the government or other authority who
discourages over-eagerness or impulse. And it is also the 'general
public' who ignores, rejects or censures such precocity.

Nonetheless, a few mild days (or, in human effort, a few
lucky breaks from our friend Jupiter) and plant and animal life
are already awakening, so that steps have to be taken to protect the growth from the generally severe conditions. Capricorn
may be the stern mother but she is also an anxious one, well
aware of the responsibilities of parenthood, at both a personal
and social level.

In the first week of January ... sometimes so many as ... twenty
species of ... flowering plants are ... unnaturally in bloom ...
   Urged by hunger, millions upon millions [of birds] come pouring
down upon us from the frozen realms of the north, where the sources of
vegetable life are completely locked up ...
(THE FARMER'S DICTIONARY)

And it is again necessary, as in the previous Earth sign of
Virgo, for hard work and organisation. Not only to ensure
that animals and plants (and humans) are protected against the
freezing conditions and have food to eat, but also to ensure
future prosperity.

In January [some] ewes begin to lamb, and require an unusual degree of
care ... On enclosed farms ... cattle should be well attended to ...
The thrashing should be so proportioned ... as to make the supply of
straw ... always sufficient ... The winter fattening of cattle is at the
busiest in January and may be conducted ... by placing the food in
mangers under open sheds ... or by giving it in the house in the
manner of strict stall-feeding.   (THE FARMER'S DICTIONARY)

At the Summer Solstice, in the sign of Cancer, the motivation to protect is emotional and personal. In Capricorn,
which is a social and earthy sign, the motivation stems from
practicality and expedience. Cancer/Capricorn, like all pairs
of opposites, affect and depend on each other. Cancer is the
'family', Capricorn the 'establishment'; it is the society, the
corporation, the nation that was begun in Libra, incubated in
Scorpio, expanded in Sagittarius, and manifested as a complete
entity in Capricorn. The Cancerian can function in society and
in a businesslike way. Similarly, the Capricornian sense of duty
can, in individuals, be coloured by emotionally protective urges.
(Clara Barton, founder of the Red Cross, was a Capricornian.)
   The family-type structures of a corporation, or a country,
reflect this polar dependence. The personal family is also a
hierarchy and the home itself is moulded into concrete form
and style by the structuring qualities and social influence of
Capricorn.
   In Cancer, the individual is the mother. In Capricorn, the

board of directors, or government, is the 'mother'. And this mother has to run her 'family' as efficiently as any mother must run her family unit. Society's laws, invented and enforced in Sagittarius and refined and extended in Capricorn, protect the individual. But they are not made *for* the individual. In this last third of the zodiac the collective entity is all-important and it is the integrity of this greater organism that Capricorn feels constrained to maintain.

The Capricorn archetype is the perfect society, creating and created by the perfect government. Governments and societies, being made up of individuals, are generally incapable of sustaining the wideness of vision necessary to fulfil such an ideal. Even so, the individual is overshadowed by the power of the archetype, and whether or not he or she fulfils this highest ideal, personal feelings and needs will often be overruled. In practice, this can make the government or other corporate-type entity seemingly cold and impersonal — of necessity. (This is the principle of the sign, though not necessarily the style of an individual Capricorn.)

The most significant fact about Capricorn is that it is the sign in which we have chosen to place the birth of Christ — although, of course, this was not done on purpose. (Incidentally, the Sun is situated almost directly in line with the pulsating heart of our galaxy approximately three days before this date.) Christians regard Christ as their spiritual saviour and, coincidentally, India — ruled by Capricorn — is similarly regarded as the 'spiritual womb' of the world, 'the guru of the nations'.

When a thick covering of snow blankets the world (and snow is synonymous with Christmas), it too creates the sensation of a womb. Not the warm darkness of the Cancerian womb but one in which whitened sky meets whitened earth and cocoons us in a muted frozen crystal cradle that inhibits growth rather than encourages it. However, in so doing, it *preserves*, and thereby sustains the promise of new life (such as was promised with the birth of Christ).

Capricorn has more connotations of spirituality than any other sign, yet she is given the most earthy, material nature to work with. Material forces attract her because her function is to define what each thing is, and to determine its function in the greater whole. She accomplishes this task by limiting the forces of life at this time so that each object can complete its development before it is released into the world to fulfil its role or function. (Just as the child in the womb is, ideally, constrained until it has all the necessary faculties to survive in the outside world.)

Capricorn's rulership of maturity makes her uncomfortable with youth and more relaxed and confident the older she gets. She often turns prematurely grey — perhaps in anticipation of age, or because her roots lie beneath the snow!

Capricorn's ruling planet is Saturn, who is Chronos, or Father Time. He strictly metes out due 'punishment' (that is, 'failure'), if proper and due care has not been taken, as well as just reward — success, accolade and financial remuneration — if it has. In this sense, although Father Time is as impersonally severe as Nature, he is also akin to the other 'Father' (of Christmas), who, incidentally, is also capable of surprising severity: 'be good, or no presents'! The gifts that come from Capricorn endure because they are the result of patience, determination and self-discipline. In the end, Capricorn's greatest gifts may well be the satisfaction, self-respect and confidence gained on the way to attaining one's goals.

Capricorn's concern with the step-by-step construction of the scaffolding of life gives us the building industry and all those connected with it, including the management and business sides (for example, real estate management and development).

At another level, this interest with the framework of life connects the sign with the sciences and with metaphysics. Her eye for structural elegance produces architects, sculptors and artists (Leonardo da Vinci and Michelangelo are both said to have had Capricorn ascendants), as well as musicians — at least those musicians who are also composers (Beethoven had three planets in Capricorn and John Lennon the Moon).

Capricorn is the one who takes hold of life, of matter, and organises it into a form that will stand up against all adversities and trials, whether it be a building, a society, a relationship, a human being, or a set of values or beliefs. (Christianity for example, is very much a Capricorn religion inasmuch as its various forms have withstood some two thousand years of buffeting.)

Capricorn is specifically linked with the knees, and the skeleton, in the human form — on which rests our 'upstand-ingness', or our capacity to 'take a stand'.

In January, a whim of Nature may bring a warmer spell of weather, which can prematurely lure the embryo out of its earthy womb. So if Capricorn can trust only that which she is absolutely sure of, it is because she senses that the survival of all in her charge may be threatened by what turns out to be only a passing phase.

However, her caution as well as her confidence in only the proven ways may develop into a rigidity which creates in humanity its fear and mistrust of change, of the new and unproven.

Capricorn's connection with the bones and joints links it with arthritis and a progressively worsening limitation of mobility of the joints affected. This disease is a physical sym-bol, or manifestation, of the Capricornian crystallisation of viewpoint and attitude because of the fear to trust in the new and different.

Nonetheless, Capricorn is the great Tradition. It is that truth which has been tried and tested by Father Time himself and which is the firm footing our pioneers can secure on their steady climb (like the sure-footed goat that is Capricorn's emblem) to humanity's unknown evolutionary heights.

AQUARIUS

AIR (20 JANUARY–18 FEBRUARY)

In summer-time one never really knows how beautiful are the forms of the deciduous trees. It is only in winter, when they are bare of leaves, that one can fully enjoy their splendid structure and design, their admirable qualities of duly apportioned strength and grace of poise, and

*the way the spread of the many-branched head has its equivalent in the
wide-reaching ground-grasp of the root. And it is interesting to see how,
in the many different kinds of tree, the same laws are always in force,
and the same results occur, and yet by the employment of what varied
means. For nothing in the growth of trees can be much more unlike
than the habit of the oak and that of the weeping willow, though the
unlikeness only comes from the different adjustment of the same sources
of power and the same weights, just as in the movement of wind-blown
leaves some flutter and some undulate, while others turn over and back
again. Old apple-trees are specially noticeable for their beauty in winter,
when their extremely graceful shape, less visible when in loveliness of
spring bloom or in rich bounty of autumn fruit, is seen to fullest
advantage.*

(THE GARDENER'S ESSENTIAL)

Gertrude Jekyll's description of her garden once again
reinforces in superb and poetic symmetry the correspondence between sign characteristics and the seasons.

February is as naked as the truth it depicts. And Aquarius's
most fundamental goal is to know these elementary truths. To
the Aquarian, Truth is Beauty and Beauty, therefore, depends
on the balance, harmony and grace of the bare bones of existence, of the shape that underlies and defines the flesh, the
character, the society. Aquarius and Capricorn share a common
ruling planet — Saturn.

As already described, this planet is connected with structural
frameworks. For Capricorn, the order that is discovered in
these inspires a sense of security and fulfils the need to know
that of which each thing is made; including its boundaries and
limitations, in order to control its progress so that it can safely
reach its goal of perfection. Aquarius branches off in another
direction (and this is typical of Aquarius). He is more detached
in his observations than Capricorn, he is more curious and
appreciative of the differences of line and form of each object,
while yet appreciating that there is a network of underlying
connections uniting all through a common lineage with the
earth.

Where fellow creatures are concerned, Aquarius generally tolerates and accepts their idiosyncracies because he understands and appreciates the unusual and unexpected in human nature. At the same time his appreciation of the unseen web of interweaving relationships between human beings and Nature, across the globe, is a revelation of the fraternity of humanity and of the essential unity within the cosmos.

This sign's symbol is the 'water-bearer': a man with an urn, pouring out the 'water of life'. (In Egypt he was equated with Hapi, the God of the Nile, who each year brought life to the land and its people with its flooding.) There are various interpretations of what this 'water of life' represents. One of them, which seems well suited to the Aquarian nature, is the simple humanity of the sign. In this respect there is, I feel, a connection with Eros, who in his earlier form was one of the originating principles of the universe (along with Chaos, Gaea and Tartarus). Leo, Aquarius's opposite sign, is the more personal and better-known aspect of Eros: passionate love, the love for one. Aquarius is the all-embracing abstract concept: impersonal caring, or the love for many.

The accepted rulers of this sign are Saturn — which has already been mentioned in connection with the preceding sign of Capricorn — and the other ruler is Uranus. In comparison with most of the Greek gods, little was said of Uranus. He was too remote, too inaccessible to human beings. He was the sky god, the God of the Heavens.

According to Gertrude Jekyll, in *The Gardener's Essential*: '[In February] age seems to give [the bramble leaves] a sort of hard surface and enough of a polish to reflect the sky ...'

Uranus was created by, and married to, Gaea, 'Matter' or Mother Earth. Together they produced the six Titans (including Saturn/Father Time) and six Titanesses, as well as many other offspring. In fact there were so many that Gaea began to tire of it and conspired with their son, Saturn, who alone dared to attack and castrate his father. (Saturn, the force that defines the boundaries of each object in time and space, is understandably affronted by such a blatant disregard for order and discipline, which Uranus represents.)

In this respect, Saturn's rulership of Aquarius is more than just an association. It curbs in humanity any desire to ignore the restrictions set by our earthly existence and our social conventions. Aquarius is the anarchist, the rebel, the reformer. Yet he also has a fundamental need to feel he is an intrinsic part of his society, culture, peer or other group. This is what keeps him sufficiently in line to function in his world. (The planet Uranus defiantly rotates on its side and as a result technically rotates 'backwards' — going completely against the order of the rest of the solar system. Nonetheless, it remains a part of this system and must fit in with those of its laws which keep the system intact.)

By putting everything in sequence, Saturn/Time gives order to our existence. Time governs thought insofar as we can think only one thought at a time, and where each thought or idea leads reasonably to the next it gives rise to logic. The Aquarian's thought processes move so fast they, in effect, and like the principle of Uranus, transcend time. Like the computer that Aquarius rules, he can arrive at an answer way ahead of everyone else. However, because the logical sequence of his thinking has not been apparent, his answer can seem irrational — until everyone else has caught up, which in some instances could take years. Many Aquarians are in fact so far ahead of their time, and even of themselves, that they have gained a reputation for eccentricity and unconventionality.

His field of vision, like that of the Uranus of mythology, is as wide as the boundless skies, which makes it hard for him to work systematically. This can be his weakness, causing him to miss the mark occasionally, and even drastically, for his inspiration tends to work erratically like the flashes of lightning that Uranus also represents in his role as 'awakener' (bearing in mind that I have equated thunder with Aquarius's opposite sign, Leo). This means that in some area of his life he will be disorganised, leaping randomly from this idea/point/object to that. Even so, he will usually arrive at his ultimate goal sooner or later. Unless, of course, he changes direction altogether.

The Aquarian stereotypes are the bohemian, the radical, or the brilliant but absent-minded oddball scientist or professor.

(Thomas Edison was an Aquarian, Einstein had Jupiter in this sign and Carl Jung had Aquarius rising.)

> *The weather of February in any one year may be extremely variable; and that of this month in different years sometimes exhibits the most discrepant and even opposite characters. In a general view, it is a fitful succession of frosts and thaws, of drenching rains, violent storms, and genial calms; yet it may in one year be nearly all stern frost — and in another, nearly all genial and vernal mildness.*
>
> (THE FARMER'S DICTIONARY)

Similarly, the Aquarian is one moment friendly, sympathetic, the next preoccupied, remote. Any tendency to contrariness is aggravated by the repression of his feelings — feelings being so alien to this airy, intellectual sign. He may say and do the unexpected to shake people out of their complacency or even just to be different. But as shock tactics frequently provoke strong emotional responses, they can also be a means for him to live out vicariously the feelings he has so much difficulty experiencing himself.

It is not surprising that the average Aquarian is wide open, naive and defenceless where his emotions are concerned. Here in the second half of the zodiac, which is connected with the feminine principle — the unconscious, the collective — the feelings that threaten to engulf him come from a much deeper level than merely the personal. In a sense, human evolution is in the safekeeping of Aquarius. The sky god (that is, the rational, thinking mind) works with the Sun (Leo's ruler, which relates to self-awareness) to evaporate the waters of the primordial ocean, to save us from drowning in the fathomless depths of our primeval instincts and the feelings they engender. Then, when impersonality and intellect lead us too far into an arctic wasteland, Aquarius as the merciful water-bearer dispenses his 'water of love', which, in the words of the great poet, 'droppeth as the gentle rain from Heaven' to soothe and comfort the soul on its path towards the glacial peaks of pure intelligence.

To many, the Aquarian ideal of truth is a sterile kind of beauty, and we generally prefer the less ideal, but more comfortable version, coloured humanly by emotional and personal considerations. Few of us like to feel, particularly in our closer relationships, that we are objects under a microscope. Nor do we like to feel we are merely one of many — which can happen with an Aquarian partner or friend who, like the originating principle of love, differentiates between none who are in need.

There are many implications for humanity at large in this Greek myth of primordial genesis. But for the Aquarian individual in particular it is the distance and solitude, the aloneness he can at times feel. His spirit may be truly 'universal' but he is human and has feelings like the rest of us, even though he may not be comfortable with them. Yet how does one touch the sky? Leo, Aquarius's opposite sign, excels in close relationships because he is by nature fiery — warm, personal and exclusively focused on the other individual, if only subjectively. Aquarius, on the other hand, being objective, airy, rational, impartial — the very principle of 'pure intellect' — does not at all wish to be sullied or distorted by murky emotion. The diamond must remain flawless.

Like the buoy that floats on the surface of the water, he cannot immerse himself easily in his feelings, which is similar to all the airy signs, who tend to feel that they are, literally, drowning when overwhelmed by the forces of emotion. For the Aquarian even anger becomes a cold withdrawal rather than the passionate release of emotion it is for so many of us. The Rev. John M. Wilson advises for this month:

> *Top-dressings may now be spread upon grass lands; but . . . ought to . . . be of a nature which will sink into the soil, there to undergo slow chemical decomposition, and not be speedily dissipated into aeriform conditions by lying in immediate contact with the atmosphere.*
>
> (THE FARMER'S DICTIONARY)

Psychologically speaking, when we start to think about what we are feeling, we stop experiencing the feeling; we distance ourselves from it so that it is unable to penetrate, enrich and change us. This is the danger for the water-bearer, who carries and dispenses these waters, but is separate from them.

In the highest sense, the Aquarian way of relating is ideal because in its purest form it is untainted by subjective needs. Hence the fuss about the 'Aquarian Age' we are entering. This does not, of course, mean that Aquarius cannot have a close relationship. However, if he is the mating type, in the end he prefers the long-standing relationship where shared interests, loyalty and friendship are the order, rather than the clinging possessiveness, the turmoil and game-playing of being 'in love'. Like the air, he needs space, needs to circulate freely.

Aquarius is both Uranus (detached and independent) and Gaea, Mother Earth, who feels such a responsibility for all her children, for in February's changeable weather

> *stock ewes now begin to lamb, and must be very carefully attended. The shepherd ought, throughout the lambing season, to sleep close to the flock, that he may be ready to tend and assist any ewes which he sees near lambing, and may, if necessary, give the lambs some warm cow's milk.*   (THE FARMER'S DICTIONARY)

This tender sympathy for young things, either helpless or in pain, often makes of Aquarius (and the following sign, Pisces), a doctor, nurse, or other health care attendant. It also draws Aquarius into social welfare and ecology.

> *Sheep which are feeding on turnips ought now to receive oil cake, not only for their own sake, but for the benefiting of the land. All live stock now require special attention; for, in February and March, they are usually more liable to disease and damage than in any other part of the year ... Great care ought to be used ... to keep the beasts of the farm-yard constantly, cleanly, and abundantly, littered; and if the stock of straw or other litter ... appear to be insufficient ... agreement ought immediately to be made with some more provident neighbour for a regular weekly supply.*   (THE FARMER'S DICTIONARY)

Thus the eleventh sign of the zodiac gives to humanity our concern with ensuring that each part of the whole receives equal opportunity and an equal share of life's bounties.

This constant concern with equality, and the friendly impartiality of the sign, reflects his internal sense of an original Unity before its division created the eternal conflict between all opposites. This colours the Aquarian nature, and sometimes imbues his form, with an androgynous quality. There is an affinity here with the ancient Greeks who worshipped the perfectness of form in the boy youth because his shape as near as humanly possible (to the male observer) reflected the 'whole-ness' of an as yet undivided psyche, which puberty makes it impossible to deny.

Art and music are also fields of Aquarian interest and talent. Aquarius is associated with the 'air waves' and with electricity, which combines with Leo, the polar opposite sign's connection with drama and entertainment, to give us radio and television. Like Leo, Aquarius produces many actors with a particularly magnetic appeal: Clark Gable, James Dean, Farrah Fawcett, Tom Selleck — which is not surprising, given the influence of Eros who was regarded by Hesiod, a Greek writer of around 750 B.C., as being: 'Love, most beautiful of all the deathless gods. He makes men weak, he overpowers the clever mind and tames The Spirit in the breasts of men and gods?'

Using the Aquarian medium, the air waves, Leo endeavours to appeal to our sense of pleasure and fun, to evoke and inten-sify our emotions by playing out the full spectrum of human experience from soap operas to Shakespeare.

However, the fact that an art form may help to heal the human spirit is not always sufficient for Aquarius, who at a practical level can feel pressured by the enormous amount of human need and suffering. Consequently, many Aquarians feel guilty when they concentrate for too long solely on what they see as the fulfilment of their own 'selfish' needs. The Aquarian form of entertainment will often tend to convey a message, such as in a documentary about the suffering or the afflicted. Here, the aim is not to give personal enjoyment or emotional fulfilment but to awaken a sense of fraternity and responsibility to the collective whole.

If the Aquarian actor, entertainer or public figure is not actually making the documentaries, he or she will often use fame and charisma to accomplish the same goals in other ways. Aquarians can be found as organisers, spokespersons or supporters of humanitarian groups or causes — anywhere where the individual needs are subsumed to those of the needy group, or of the whole of humankind.

Leo, the Sun, the Centre, is the individual 'father' — the 'man' of the family. Aquarius is the 'family of man' — 'man' in this context being neutral, human, whole, undivided, united.

In the end, Aquarius is the Spirit of Hope, because at some time during the month of February, as Gertrude Jekyll in *The Gardener's Essential* says: '. . . the day always comes, and with it the glad certainty that summer is nearing, and that the good things promised will never fail.'

PISCES

WATER (19 FEBRUARY–20 MARCH)

Pisces is that first 'ocean' which the Greeks named Chaos — eternal night, that infinite abyss where no laws of time or space or matter isolate one plane of existence, nor any one object, from the next.

Aquarius strives for unity through equality of the parts; Pisces equalises by dissolving all boundaries so that the parts can be fused into one, thus returning each to its original undifferentiated state, to its source.

To Pisces, this complete fusion of all into one, is to return to the great womb and therefore to safety. It also means intoxication by an unspeakable, ineffable, unbearable poignance by which she is tantalised incessantly and driven restlessly to seek. However, to the human ego and mind, which craves precision and order and perceives life itself as structure and form, this same realm threatens loss of sanity, because it means extinction of the boundaries that define the self. Hence, Pisces — and its ruling planet, Neptune — hold some threat for that aspect of human nature.

The last sign of the zodiac, and the last phase of development in Nature before the cycle begins again, is therefore a cloudy, turbulent chaos. So along come the March winds to

blow away these mists of confusion so that the new life —
Aries — poised ready to burst free from the underworld, can
emerge with absolute clarity of purpose.

> *March is usually characterised as the windiest month in the year; yet it*
> *very frequently partakes of the same fickleness, uncertainty, and*
> *contrasts of character as February. Storms and strong gales occasionally*
> *blow at all times of the month . . . In most years, the prevailing wind*
> *. . . is keen, cutting, unhealthy, dry, and powerfully evaporating; but in*
> *other years, it . . . is accompanied with excessive rains . . .*
>
> (THE FARMER'S DICTIONARY)

The ruling planets of Pisces are Neptune (Poseidon), God
of the Seas, who could call up a gale or a tempest at will, and
Jupiter (Zeus), God of Storms.

Here in the last sign of the zodiacal wheel the memory of
the great cosmic tides of Earth's primordial ocean are embedded
in the cells of every living thing, working the seasons, and the
minds, hearts and lives of humanity. Where Aquarius reflects
the arctic lucidity of pure, crystalline intelligence, Pisces is the
opaque humidity of turbid emotion that wells up rhythmically
from the depths of the collective soul.

The unpredictable and erratic habits associated with February
weather and Aquarian behaviour are due to a change of mind
— this being an airy sign. Piscean changeability, on the other
hand, is due to an excess of feeling, which is expressed as
moodiness. Like the tides of the ocean, she is one moment
outgoing, optimistic, confident, exuberant and the next she is
withdrawn, timid, morose, apathetic. Some Pisceans favour
more of one mood than the other, although most will swing
frequently from one extreme to the other.

The more exuberant Piscean finds it difficult to face the
'real world' because everything seems so dull. This type craves
the same vivid intensity of colour in her life as that which occurs
beneath the green and turquoise tropical oceans. Here Nature
herself is larger than life, more beautiful, wondrous, romantic
and magical. The colours associated with the Piscean planets
range from purple — which belongs to Jupiter, King of the Gods

— through the mauves and lilacs of gentle compassion to the deepest turquoise blues associated with Neptune. The Earth too seems to try to express these hues during this season.

> *In early March many and lovely are the flowering bulbs, and among them a wealth of blue, the more precious that it is the colour least frequent among flowers. The blue of* Scilla sibirica, *like all blues that have in them a suspicion of green, has a curiously penetrating quality; the blue of* Scilla bifolia *does not attack the eye so smartly.* Chionodoxa sardensis *is of a full and satisfying colour ...* Chionodoxa Luciliœ *... varies greatly; one may pick out light and dark blue, and light and dark of almost lilac colour ... and ... no flower of the whole year can show a more splendid and sumptuous colour than the purple of* Iris reticulata *... some nearer blue, and some reddish purple, but the type remains the best garden flower.* Iris stylosa *... gives flower from November till mid-April, the strongest rush of bloom being about the third week in March. It is a precious plant ... delicately scented, of a tender and yet full lilac-blue ... Beyond ... is the ... thin wood of young silver Birch and Holly, in summer clothed below with bracken, but now bristling with the bluish spears of Daffodils and the buds that will soon burst into bloom.*
>
> (THE GARDENER'S ESSENTIAL)

But the glorious and extravagant vision fades behind the veil of everyday existence, which to Pisces can become as insipid as the intensely hued coral when it is removed from the deceptive enhancement of its watery habitat.

The other type and mood of Pisces is more delicate and vulnerable, in a world that seems too gross and crude for her fine sensitivities. This too is reflected in Nature at this time.

> *... below, the fading rust of the now nearly flattened fronds of last year's bracken, and the still paler drifts of leaves from neighbouring Oaks and Chestnuts ... The grass is barely green as yet, but has the faint winter green of herbage not yet grown and still powdered with the short remnants of the fine-leaved, last-year-mown heath grasses. Brown leaves still hang on young Beech and Oak ...*
>
> *The nearly related combination of colour is a delight to the trained colour-eye. There is nothing brilliant; it is all restrained, refined, in*

> *harmony with the veiled light that reaches the flowers through the great*
> *clumps of Hollies and tall half-overhead Chestnuts and neighbouring*
> *Beech. The colours are all a little 'sad,' as the old writers so aptly say*
> *of the flower-tints of secondary strength. But it is a perfect picture. One*
> *comes to it again and again as one does to any picture that is good to*
> *live with . . .* (THE GARDENER'S ESSENTIAL)

This less resilient type of Piscean is equally disillusioned when harsh reality emerges from the gentle, softening haze of her fantasy. Yet it is out of this poignant sadness that her poetic and artistic inspiration arise.

The Piscean imagination is difficult to comprehend by those not blessed — and cursed — with it, because she can transcend all boundaries, cross all dimensions and even touch the stars, at least momentarily. It is the Piscean phase in the cyclical course of development that gives to humanity its wildest fancies, its impossible utopias, and allows it to taste, fleetingly at least, the golden nectar of divine ecstasy and madness — a moment of freedom to create and spend in our ivory towers, without which we might perish in the banal.

The glamorous world of theatre and cinema, where special effects can take us into fantastic worlds we might never otherwise have known, is one of her media. Samuel Goldwyn and Walt Disney both had Neptune culminating overhead when they were born. Sydney Poitier, Elizabeth Taylor, Liza Minelli all have Sun in Pisces. Audrey Hepburn, Frank Sinatra have the Moon there. Robert Redford has Pisces Ascending, and Sally Field has Neptune on the Ascendant.

Examples in the field of imaginative writing are Edgar Allan Poe with Mercury in Pisces and Charles Dickens with Venus in that sign. The poet Shelley had the Moon in Pisces, while some musical examples are Chopin with the Sun here, and George Harrison with the Sun and Venus. Artists such as Cézanne had the Moon in Pisces, while Van Gogh had Venus and Mars.

It is obvious from these few examples that if the strong influence of Pisces or Neptune occurs in the chart of a writer, actor, film-maker, artist or musician, she or he is likely to become at least popular, if not idolised. Due to the Piscean openness to the undercurrent of collective moods and feelings, she is responsive to trends and fashions while they are in the process of forming. If they have the necessary skills, those influenced strongly by this sign and its ruling planet are able to express concretely for us all our deepest feelings and yearnings, of which we ourselves may not as yet be aware. So we find ourselves saying of the book, movie, character, music or painting ... Yes, that's it!

Just as Pisces can be the idol, so may she lay herself at the feet of some guru, god or goddess, in enraptured surrender. In fact, Pisces can adore and worship anyone whom she feels has special qualities, attaching herself as a puppy to its master or mistress. In personal relationships too she will idealise her partner who, sooner or later, since he or she is human, will likely fall from the pedestal of perfection and purity, leaving Pisces characteristically broken-hearted, disillusioned and frustrated.

Her contact with that 'something' which at moments causes her spirit to soar, commits her to a lifelong quest for ways to prolong the ecstasy. If other ways are not open to her, she may seek to satiate her yearning via opiate means, where the 'beautiful illusion' is re-created synthetically. A small quantity of the Piscean substances, such as alcohol or narcotics, grants the desired euphoria and distances her from reality enough to numb the pain, relieve the ennui, make life acceptable. The more imbibed, the more exposed she is to the state of the collective psyche.

This may be at least one of the reasons why a dependence on alcohol or drugs can lead to an increasingly negative state of mind. Women, in particular, who by their very nature are more open to collective and instinctual levels of feeling, are generally more at risk. For men, the initial sweet surrender as the sensual waters of feeling enfold them, may provide a temporary release from the cold prison of the rational intellect, as well as from life's unceasing demands. Naturally, the danger of dependence exists for all.

Pisces has dominion over all substances that produce a change in consciousness, or induce withdrawal from ordinary consciousness. These principles also link the sign with places of retreat or confinement, such as monasteries, prisons and sanatoriums. The influence of Pisces' opposite sign, Virgo, connects Pisces with formal medicines and drugs particularly, such as morphine, pethidine, anaesthetics, and of course with the places in which these are used, such as hospitals.

Another look at agricultural activities at this time shows many similarities to February, when farm creatures were in need of extra special care, just as they are in March.

Ewes in particular ought to be transferred, along with their young, to sound new grass; and they should be kept in a warm, dry, well sheltered, and perfectly clean *condition. All cows and mares which have quite recently produced young, should be carefully and nicely attended to, for food, for shelter, and especially for ventilation and thorough* cleanliness *... Poultry, during March, require much attention; their boxes ... should be so often replenished with hay ... as to secure perfect* cleanliness; *their houses should be so* cleansed *and lime-washed as to be kept free from vermin; their ... food, should be good and regular; and free access ought to be constantly afforded them to a gravelled yard, to* clean *water ... The turnip fallow should now be thoroughly stirred,* cleaned *... The rising wheat crops ought, without any delay, to be* cleaned *...*

(THE FARMER'S DICTIONARY; emphasis added).

This concept of course is well corresponded with the Piscean connection with hospitals and health care. The individual Piscean can be imprecise, disordered, untidy and unkempt, but she can also be fussy to the point of making a fetish about cleanliness, at least in some part of her life.

The Piscean openness and richness of feeling often give her an internal sense of abundance which fills her to overflowing and permeates all levels of her existence. One result of this is that she has a tendency to cry easily. Another, which at least the Capricornians of the world will criticise, is that she can be overindulgent and wasteful in the extreme.

> *In March, all sheep . . . require to be extremely well kept; for if they*
> *be insufficiently fed or carelessly tended at this season, all the money*
> *previously expended on them will be nearly thrown away . . .*
> *Throughout the month, all cows and . . . cattle should be kept close in*
> *the farm-yards, and on no account allowed to wander over any of the*
> *fields; for, when they find their way into a grassfield, they not only*
> *break the sward and make a waste . . . but, by obtaining a mouthful or*
> *two of sweet young grass, contract a repugnance to the dry and*
> *somewhat artificial food of the yards.*

(THE FARMER'S DICTIONARY)

Pisces is probably the least logical sign. Her thoughts are based purely on her feelings. Consequently, she does not usually do well in head-on confrontations. This leads her to go about getting what she wants with more subtle methods. If she is a clever Pisces, her opponents will end up utterly confounded by her arguments. And the more logical and rational their reasoning the more confused they will be, because Pisces' knowledge and understanding is not learned. It arises spontaneously from the depths of her psyche . . . from the heart of Chaos, where all paradoxes are true. The careful order of existence created by Virgo, Pisces' opposite sign, is here scattered and dissolved, leaving Pisces forced to face the future with blind faith.

Pisces marks the end of the cycle. She stands at the door of a new world with her feet in the ashes of the old one, unable to pass through. She is a visionary. She knows in the very roots of her being that in the dying coals of the old fire lie the smouldering embers that will ignite new and even greater blazes to illumine the progress of humanity and inspire it with its warmth and light.

Having reached this final point, having suffered 'beneath the wheel' enables Pisces to identify with others and envelop them with empathetic emotion. Pisces is the symbol for one of humanity's greatest virtues. Not the motherliness associated with Cancer, nor the warmth and generosity of spirit of Leo, nor even the selfless brotherly sympathy and concern of Aquarius. Pisces stands for compassionate love — the ultimate 'morality' — born of the suffering experienced in the wearying and enlightening pilgrim's progress through the eleven preceding phases, and the sacrifice that must be made at the end.

Pisces is the Saviour, the redeemer of lost souls. The current Piscean Age more or less began with the best-known saviour of our times — Jesus Christ. Because Pisces experiences the suffering of others as if it were her own, she feels compelled to save. She will champion, serve and redeem the downtrodden, the sick, the weak, the underdog. And she will literally take in every stray that crosses her path, be it human or animal.

This compulsion to save people — from themselves if necessary, which is not always welcome — draws many Pisceans into the fields of religion and healing. But it also makes of her a 'soft touch', vulnerable to any sob story, and eventually often the victim as well as the saviour.

In essence, Pisces is the whole which must now be sacrificed to the future. And it is this sense of finality, of dissolution, which pervades the Piscean on an unconscious level and which lies at the roots of her tendency to be easily disheartened. (Her classic catchphrase being: 'what's the point?')

> ... at any time during the month when the wind is in the east or north-east, all increase and development of vegetation appears to cease. As things are, so they remain. Plants that are in flower retain their bloom, but, as it were, under protest. A kind of sullen dullness pervades all plant life. Sweet-scented shrubs do not give off their fragrance; even the woodland moss and earth and dead leaves withhold their sweet, nutty scent. The surface of the earth has an arid, infertile look; a slight haze of an ugly grey takes the colour out of objects in middle distance, and seems to rob the flowers of theirs, or to put them out of harmony with all things around ...   (THE GARDENER'S ESSENTIAL)

Pisces both precedes and ends all things. It is the crown of every moment that has gone before since the very first atoms formed, coalesced and grew, and humanity arose from the cosmic dusts. And it is the foundation for every moment that follows into the infinite future. The Pisces symbol of two fishes chasing each other's tails is the symbol of resurrection and immortality, the never-ending circle of Life. So it is inevitable that ...

... a day comes, or, perhaps, a warmer night, when the wind, now breathing gently from the south-west, puts new life into all growing things. A marvellous change is wrought in a few hours. A little warm rain has fallen, and plants, invisible before, and doubtless still underground, spring into glad life. (THE GARDENER'S ESSENTIAL)

PART III

FUNCTION

1 USES

PREDICTION

The astrologer's reputation usually depends on the accuracy of his or her predictions. However, precision in astrological prediction is often only a matter of chance. This is mainly because each symbol in a horoscope can have a wide variety of meanings, based on how that symbol relates to the other symbols and also on the individual's personal and unique background. So, how current or future influences will affect you depends on your innate nature and your past. It is a situation similar to that of a psychologist interpreting the symbols in a patient's dreams: the more comprehensive and intimate the practitioner's knowledge of the person, the more accurate will be the interpretation of the symbols. Similarly, the better your astrologer knows you, the more precise the predictions can be.

For example, suppose there is an imminent influence in your horoscope that implies greatly increased activity in your life. If you are a naturally active person this would be more likely to result in a rash action or overactivity than if you are naturally relaxed or timid.

In the latter instance such an influence could mean that you will simply feel more motivated than usual. Then again it would evoke a different response in someone who has recently experienced a period of frustration, compared to the way he or she would react after a period of freedom and success.

If astrological forecasts are approached with an open mind but in full awareness of the astrologer's human nature — that is, his or her ability to make mistakes — astrological prediction can be most helpful in many situations. It can present to you a different, yet authentic view of your problems, thereby giving you a better chance of developing an alternative course of action — if that is what you want. If not, it can show you a more positive side to the situation, pinpointing the facets of your character it is strengthening and developing, and perhaps even to what end. It can warn you of impending trouble spots in work, health, relationships, family or finances. It can prepare you for times when, due to limiting circumstances for example, it might be better for you to consolidate rather than to expand. Conversely, it can ready you for potential opportunities so that you can make the most of them. But most importantly of all, it can help you discover the underlying reasons for the conditions in your life so that you can understand their psychological basis: the root cause, rather than merely the effect, the symptom.

HORARY ASTROLOGY

Horoscopes are often set up for the moment an idea is mentally formulated or put into action. This is called 'horary' astrology. And it works for the same reason that natal astrology works: because the potential inherent in the moment a human being is born can also be present in the moment of the birth of an idea or of the inception of some new process or, in fact, at any beginning.

The chart erected for such a birth mirrors the state of our (near) universe at that moment and from the viewpoint of that place. In effect, all the planetary positions and relationships are caught in a photographic still. The innate characteristics of that moment are 'set' in the form of the object manifesting through that point in time and space. However, in life nothing stays the same; a human being (and equally an action or idea) whose first moment was 'captured' within the horoscope, perpetually grows and changes. The map that we examine to assess a human being's potential is really only a means of analysing and assessing a *moment's potential* within the context of the perpetual flow of time. Each moment derives from the one before it and is the matrix from which the next moment is born, and inherent in each moment is its past and its future. Consequently, this provides a basis for assessing the future of a particular objective, situation or action.

In order to obtain the most accurate results it is important to have a horary chart drawn up at a time that is specially relevant to the future of the action or idea. An astrologer will pick the most pertinent moment as being either the time the idea was conceived; the first move was made or, should it be a relationship matter, when you first met the individual. If you cannot recall the exact moment, the astrologer will choose the time you posed the question. These moments are culminations or energy peaks with regard to the matter concerned.

Horary charts have the widest range of all astrological charts, mainly because they are simple and totally relevant to the issue at hand. They are even used to find missing persons or lost articles. And in the form of a chart called a 'solar return', they are set up for the minute the Sun returns to the exact degree in which it was situated at the birth of the individual in question, to obtain a general picture of the coming year. They are useful in assessing world affairs, such as the outcome of elections, wars, the signing of treaties, announcements of government decisions, and so on. They can also be used to gain a better insight into past events and the circumstances surrounding them.

Should you have a question about the future of a particular idea, action, or whatever, and after setting up a chart the astrologer says he or she cannot help you, do not be concerned. It will be because the question has been asked at the 'wrong' time. That is, it is either premature, already resolved, or not as relevant as you think, even though this may not yet be apparent to you. Such situations are indicated in the chart by traditional 'signatures'; that is, by special planetary configurations or conditions, which any astrologer practised in this type of analysis will recognise. The astrologer is not trying to conceal something horrendous, because even if the signs are not propitious for the matter at hand, the astute astrologer would just issue a warning.

ELECTIONAL ASTROLOGY

This is closely related to horary astrology because it can also be used for any subject and is based on the same principles.

The difference is that with electional astrology — as the name implies — it is used to find the best moment to begin an event, rather than to assess the course of an idea by the conditions of the moment it was formulated into a question. Electional astrology is used to try to ensure that an action is begun at a time when there is as much positive energy as possible for that specific type of action. It is like the trapeze artist timing his or her leap for the moment of greatest impetus or perfect coordination that will ensure contact with another trapezist at the crucial moment.

With electional astrology, the idea is that you can plan the best possible moment to begin any special activity, such as getting married, having a surgical operation, setting out on a journey, placing an advertisement, opening a business, changing residence, buying a home, beginning speculative ventures, signing contracts, and so on. But it does not, of course, guarantee success any more than giving a horse the best jockey will make it win.

VOCATION

Someone once said that 'character is destiny'. And as the horoscope is a blueprint of individual character, in this sense it can be used as a guide to individual destiny.

One area in which destiny can be seen to culminate is in the vocation. This is usually thought of as the 'job' or 'occupation'. At best it is the 'career' or 'profession'. But there is a much deeper and wider meaning to what is after all the apex of one's ambitions. One dictionary definition of 'vocation' is: 'an inner call or summons to perform a specific function or fill a certain position, especially of a spiritual nature ...'; also: 'a divine call to a state of union or salvation with God ...' Obviously, then, a vocation is not just a 'job', unless of course one's job also happens to be one's calling.

The point is that the vocation is one of the means by which we can express our essential selves, not only for ourselves but for the society of which we are an integral part. It should therefore be our special niche, our place in the world.

Some find their paths early and without much hesitation.

Many of us, however, have at least a few false starts and a struggle to discover what our role is in life. It is difficult to be single-minded enough to find this one vital place. Often the personality has several sides demanding expression, and the doubt that this creates makes a hole into which outside influences filter and add further to the confusion.

Our minds and senses are continually assaulted by the onslaught of a myriad daily happenings, from radio, television, movies, newspapers — as well as the people in our everyday lives with whom we must interact. All this can leave us with so little time to discriminate that we cannot properly digest those personal experiences that have meaning and relevance before we are distracted and enticed by the seemingly more exciting experiences of others. It is a mammoth task just trying to keep abreast of all the personal, social and technological developments in order to relate to our world at all. In fact, much of what we think we are is all too often only a reflection of other people's experiences, thoughts and lives. Peer, parental, environmental and circumstantial pressures all influence and bias our choices.

There are several specific areas of the horoscope the astrologer will examine to find earning potentials, work aptitudes and opportunities, and career possibilities. However, unless the indications all converge without conflict — in which case the person concerned would probably not have any questions about the matter in the first place — finding the vocation as destiny is not an easy task. Also, however intuitive the astrologer may be, he or she cannot know precisely what type of, or how many, experiences are necessary for any particular person before their true or ultimate path emerges — assuming there is only one path. Sometimes, what may appear to have been the wrong path and wasted time was actually a form of preparation for some greater purpose. It might also be that the vocation is not necessarily the area of greatest earning power.

Then again, some individuals do not need a profession to feel fulfilled. It is surely as possible for a mother and housewife to be answering her 'true calling' (despite some feminist reactions against such an idea) as it is for a ballet dancer or business executive to be responding not to their destiny but to outside influences and pressures.

Yet, despite these cautions, the proper use of astrology can help an individual to find, define and integrate the various qualities, needs and leanings, as well as possible avenues for their expression. At the very least, it can give those who are confused about where they are headed in life a chance to discover what it is they specially have to contribute to the world, whether it be a product, a skill, or simply a quality of being.

CHILDREN'S HOROSCOPES

There are conflicting views in this area and I would like to present both sides of the argument so that parents can make their own decisions.

Those astrologers who are against the idea argue that even though the aim may be to assist the child's development, it actually interferes with the natural unfoldment of the child's character. A natal horoscope will expose many possibilities. But heredity will bias a few of those, and environment and experience will play an important part as to which facets of the character indicated in a horoscope will develop. Also, it is vital to take into account the 'something else' that lies beyond the scope of a horoscope: that 'essential self', or 'whole that is greater than the sum of the parts'. I would like to relate an experience which prompted this assumption.

I have come across many sets of 'astrological twins' (that is, two people who are unrelated but born on the same day and year, in different places). In one particular instance, two such women consulted me in the same week. Both were a strong mixture of Virgo and Pisces, which are opposite signs. One of the women was practical, efficient, businesslike — emphasising the Virgo qualities. The other was soft, dreamy, artistic, living in a world of her own making, and epitomising the Piscean qualities. Of course, these differences could easily be accounted for by their dissimilar backgrounds, heredity, and so on.

However, this explanation would not be relevant in the case of the biological twins, brought up by the same parents and with the same influences, lifestyles, schools, and so on. The particular twins I speak of here both have the Sun in Libra with Capricorn ascendants. In both charts, Saturn rules and is in conjunction with Neptune in the sign of Libra.

Like day and night one twin expresses the Saturn influence: career-oriented, practical, organised, while the other sister expresses much more of the Neptune qualities. She is more passive, quiet, less assertive and less confident.

Those who perceive dangers in attempting to read a child's horoscope suggest that because the child has no experience and little personality development to point the astrologer in the right direction, it is extremely difficult to predict precisely how its life and character will unfold, as the above examples illustrate. This means that in trying to deal with problems that exist only in potentiality, the child's parents could conceivably precipitate some negative or conflicting characteristic into being, which might not otherwise have manifested.

The astrologer's influence is also considered, by those who disagree with child horoscopy, as a potential interference with the child's future in that it could result in the child being encouraged along a wrong path.

Yet the arguments for having a child's horoscope interpreted are also convincing.

Parents usually consult an astrologer because they are puzzled and worried about some aspects of their children's behaviour.

However enlightened the parents are, it is not always possible for them to be able to recognise and fulfil a child's deeper needs. The reasons for this are myriad. Often the needs are not socially acceptable, or they may interfere with family harmony or principles. Perhaps the parents are not on the same emotional wavelength as the child. Or else the child simply cannot articulate his or her more essential needs. As a result, the child may express these needs in a way that to an adult may seem negative, such as in a temper tantrum.

Astrology cannot modify the child's behaviour. However, if it can reveal a tangible and logical reason as to why the child is behaving in a particular way, it can at least relieve some of the pressures on the parents. It might also help them find

natural and creative outlets for undirected energies. It follows
that if their frustrations are lessened because they understand
their child better, the chances are that the child will respond
positively because it, too, will be less frustrated. And when
the child becomes an adult, these previously 'negative' energies
may become deep fonts of strength, creativity and motivation
that lead to a happier, more satisfying life.

COMPATIBILITY

One of astrology's most valuable uses is in the area of
relationships. There are many books on the market about Sun
sign compatibility. However, although some of them are ex-
cellent introductions to this area of astrology, only a full chart
comparison can reveal the finer, more subtle qualities of a
relationship. An astrologer can, for instance, pinpoint where
one partner's energies have the potential to spark off a host
of dynamic but previously dormant talents, characteristics or
strengths in the other partner. An astrologer can also show
where each partner supports the other and contributes to his
or her growth and development.

It is good to be reminded of the positive aspects of a relationship. However, this is rarely the reason most people consult
an astrologer. What they usually want to know is why it is
not working. It is here that astrology excels, because it can
locate harmful undercurrents which may eventually destroy
what might otherwise be a fine relationship. At least it can
reassure both parties that neither — or both — are to blame,
and why.

When one considers the vast number of influences that
form our attitudes and expectations while we are young and
impressionable, it is not surprising that such undercurrents
exist in our relationships. It is even less surprising that our
emotional needs become so entangled.

While we are growing up we learn the 'rules' about love.
Some of these rules are social ones: morals and such. Others we
pick up as we go along by watching the world and its ways. Our
complicated relationships with our parents and brothers and
sisters are made more so when we step outside the relatively closed

and safe environment of the home, into society. From here we
extract further considerations, meanings, values and rules, many
of which we come to believe are the desiderata for emotional
happiness. We are led to believe the success of a relationship
depends on the degree to which the people concerned are 'in
love'. We naively accept these values — at least while we are
young.

Having struggled through this complex maze of impressions
we finally reach the point where society considers us ready to
experience love: to get married and start our own families.
Naturally, we are rarely equipped, or ready, for such a commitment.

Most people have suffered the pangs of love, whether through
experience or the lack of it. Many of us believe in fate — naturally enough — because we are influenced by movies, poetry
and novels.

The problem we confront in our relationships — and this
is where astrology comes in — is not caused by fate but for
the most part by the fact that there is a war going on inside
of us between the conscious and the unconscious selves. The
conscious self is the part we know as 'I' and the unconscious
is a part that so often ends up as being 'You'. It is the polar
opposite to what we perceive as 'I', and very often it is in
conflict with what the 'I' part thinks and wants.

This inner polarity is also bound up first with our relationships with our parents. And this is where many parts of the
horoscope come into play. Unfortunately, this subject is beyond the scope of this book — and the writer's knowledge.
However, the moderate explanation attempted here is to give
the reader at least a taste of the value, richness and understanding of our relationships that astrology can provide.

Those familiar with the works of the psychiatrist Carl Jung
would know that he spent his life studying the psyche and its
two halves: the conscious and the unconscious, how these correspond respectively with the principles of 'male' and 'female',
and how this in turn corresponds with the relationship between
'I' and 'You'. His theory and approach have become commonly
accepted and are in fact an expansion of the ancient Eastern

concept of the interplay between the positive and negative forces of the universe, commonly known as *yang* and *yin*.

Both this idea and Jung's concepts in particular are relevant to the development of astrology. The reasons for this are as follows.

Humankind has 'constellated' the twelve types of the zodiac onto the stars in the sky. To look at those star patterns, it is difficult to imagine exactly how they could have been divided into groups representing such images as a 'water-bearer' (Aquarius), a lion (Leo), or a bull (Taurus). These constellations are a product of the combined, unconscious qualities of humanity. (Jung called them 'archetypes'.)

In the same way, our personal unconscious qualities constellate themselves outside of us onto other human beings. We made the stars fit the designs we projected onto them because they are approximations of those designs. In the same way, the people to whom we are strongly attracted have qualities that so closely approximate our own unconscious characteristics that we can actually believe those people have those qualities. This usually causes us to fall in love with them or to dislike them intensely.

In the horoscope, there is a point which represents this unconscious self, or opposite polarity. It is exactly opposite the Ascendant (the degree rising on the eastern horizon at birth) — the 'I'. The opposite point is the Descendant — the degree setting in the west (corresponding with the sign of Libra), or 'You', the partner. This part of the chart is not the last and only word on the subject of polarities and the unconscious partner. However, it is nonetheless the focal point of this urge to make oneself complete by joining with another who, as closely as possible, resembles this hidden self. We have mixed feelings about this self too: we are afraid of it and dislike it intensely (therefore the seventh house also represents our open enemies); yet it has qualities we also admire, even envy.

For example, a Sagittarius-ascending person — who sees life in wholes or generalisations, who seeks the meaning behind facts and existence and who seeks to leap beyond logic and above mundane reality — will tend to gravitate towards, and be attracted to, Gemini types. Gemini deals with and gathers details and facts. Unlike Sagittarius, Gemini interacts with, and responds automatically to, his or her immediate environment instead of to some remote possibility. The person with a Sagittarian ascendant also contains Gemini within. But because it is hidden and feels alien, he or she does not want to — or cannot — consciously and freely express it. In fact, he or she will get annoyed by those traits in others.

The attraction is due to the fact that there is more to life than abstract concepts and philosophical speculations. There are everyday realities, ideas and facts that together add up to an aggregate that amounts to more than the sum of its parts. This abstract essence the Sagittarian type grasps intuitively, yet could never define without the separate elements provided by Gemini. Conversely, the Gemini preoccupation with the details and facts of life, with the day-to-day events, would make an automaton rather than a human being, without the underlying coherence which joins them together and gives this dry information a purpose and a meaning. No wonder the attraction is so compelling.

The projection of these internal contents onto another being is like looking into a mirror that we mistake for a window. The image we first see arouses an urge to possess because it reflects an inner quality that we vaguely sense we need. Unfortunately, and inevitably, the images are not as good and as beautiful as we might at first have thought. This then arouses a desire to change what we see, because if we are really only looking into a mirror we will eventually discover our own defects there — not only our charms. Ever been embarrassed by your partner's behaviour? (The real clue as to how much of ourselves we are projecting is when no one else is embarrassed.) One can come to loathe that mirror image. Then those destructive, subtle, and often unconscious, manipulations begin.

By comparing the various characteristics and needs indicated in the horoscopes of two partners (and also utilising a third chart, called a 'composite', which is a combination of the two and describes the relationship itself as a separate entity), the astrologer can find these hidden factors and bring them out into the open. Only here can an attempt be made to deal with these destructive energies on a practical everyday level.

Obviously, the relationship has a better chance of surviving if the blind spots are discovered before misunderstanding or ignorance has a chance to create rigid patterns of response towards each other. Once set, such responses can lead to irreparable rifts making the relationship a prison that either stifles the potential of both partners, or else ends in resentment and bitterness. This in turn leads to the next relationship being bound by the same patterns to a similar fate.

It would seem basic commonsense, therefore, to be wary of anyone to whom we are so compellingly magnetised. But this is a warning that will be — fruitfully — ignored because such feelings usually outweigh mere logic. After all, these are lessons learned only by experience, which is invaluable to our self-discovery, growth and transformation.

Carl Jung suggested that there are four primary ways in which we individually relate to life: some of us relate through the senses, some through the feelings, others through the mind and the rest through the intuition. These four modes have been correlated respectively with the four elements of the zodiac: earth, water, air and fire. Each of us is a mixture of these elements, though sometimes one will be missing and usually one will predominate.

The following list shows which signs are associated with each element. However, this does not mean that if your Sun is in the fiery sign of Aries you are automatically predominantly an 'intuitive' type. (I will explain why shortly.)

There are ten planets (including the Sun and Moon which are classed as planets for convenience), plus four primary angles of the natal horoscope to consider. (Ascendant, Descendant, Midheaven and Nadir/1st, 7th, 10th and 4th houses respectively). This means that although your Sun may be fire/intuitive, you might be predominantly 'mental' because of an emphasis on airy signs, or even because you are male — which, again, I will explain in a moment.

SIGN	ELEMENT	TYPE
Aries *Leo* *Sagittarius*	Fire	Intuition
Taurus *Virgo* *Capricorn*	Earth	Senses
Gemini *Libra* *Aquarius*	Air	Intellect
Cancer *Scorpio* *Pisces*	Water	Feelings

Carl Jung pointed out that each of these modes is diametrically opposed to the other:

Aries/Sagittarius/Leo (Fire/Intuition) opposes Taurus/Virgo/Capricorn (Earth/Senses).

Gemini/Libra/Aquarius (Air/Intellect) opposes Cancer/Scorpio/Pisces (Water/Feelings).

This suggests that the fiery, intuitive type will be alienated from the earthy, material side of life in some way. He or she can of course function in the material world and in practical matters but would do so through — in effect — mimicry. The purely intuitive type would not be able to relate to the sensory type's genuine need for material evidence and practical applicability of ideas because the former is away in the world of imagination, inspiration, abstraction and possibility. Meanwhile, the practical, earthy type cannot understand the intuitive type's complete lack of realism. He or she cannot relate to the intuitive type's world because there is nothing there that the earthy individual can focus on and grasp.

Similarly, the airy, rational personality would be out of touch with his or her feelings and would be unable to understand a feeling-dominant person's intensity in an argument, or their subjectivity or why they take everything so personally. On the other hand, the feeling type would become frustrated with a partner who rationalises everything and never gets impassioned about anything. Such an individual would seem superficial, insensitive and cold.

It is easy to see from these simple divisions of human nature why there are so many misunderstandings. Emotional people cannot separate their feelings from their thoughts in a personal discussion and will identify with their thoughts. Rational people, on the other hand, cannot get in touch with their feelings because they are like a buoy floating on the surface of the ocean — they may try to immerse themselves but they will keep bobbing back up to observe rather than participate. Intuitive people cannot keep their feet on the ground and practical people cannot allow their feet to leave it.

If an astrologer can explain this to two people who are in such a situation they may just be able to learn to make allowances and adjustments to cope. More importantly, each one will understand why the other acts as they do instead of believing their responses to be purposely contentious.

It is difficult for us to categorise the various elements within our relationships. The separate issues of communication, emotional interchange (which is also a form of communication, of course, but at a different level to intellectual exchange), sexual compatibility, security needs, creative expression, and so forth, all tend to merge in our view of our relationship. This happens partly because most of us are not in the habit of making such a detailed analysis and partly because if one area is weak or fails, then the other areas also tend to suffer so that the whole structure is weakened.

Each planet (including the Sun and Moon) represents a particular facet of human nature. When there are tense relationships between planets, the energies affected will be those that the particular planets signify. When there are cross-aspects between two horoscopes, they show the astrologer which areas in the relationship are particularly vulnerable.

The SUN represents the ego, the central will or individuality. Difficult aspects to the Sun from a planet in the partner's chart could result in a battle of wills. One person may try to dominate the other and in order for such a relationship to work, each will have to allow the other to carry on with their lives as they see fit. Positive aspects to the Sun suggest support for fundamental goals and confidence in each other.

The MOON represents the state of our instincts and deeply ingrained conditioning. A planet in tense aspect to the partner's Moon would spark off negative conditioned responses or instinctive rejoinders, especially when the two live together, because the Moon rules the domestic environment. Positive contacts with the Moon suggest an instinctive understanding of each other's basic needs and a desire to nurture each other.

Mercury is the planet of communication. An astrologer can discover whether communications are at cross-purposes by looking at the position of *Mercury* in the charts. If there is a difficulty, the astrologer can show ways to overcome it through other, more harmonious avenues of interchange that may be indicated in the horoscopes.

VENUS is the planet of 'relating', of love, companionship and affection, so it is of great significance in compatibility. If Venus receives friendly aspects from the partner's planets, it will go a long way towards working out differences that arise in other areas. As it also has to do with values, difficult aspects would create problems in the different value systems, or the pair may not enjoy the same forms of relaxation, or will have conflicting cultural tastes — art, music, and so on.

MARS has to do with basic energy drives, as expressed in business, sex, sport, and general motivation. Contacts with Mars in the partner's chart can result in positively combined efforts, or constant confrontations, in much mutual accomplishment, or simple frustration. Smooth aspects give a healthy tone to a relationship and add liveliness, because there tends to be cooperative effort and sexual compatibility. Difficult aspects can result in competitive and angry confrontations, because of a constant blocking of each other's drive.

JUPITER interaspects show whether there will be growth and progress or, negatively, mutual encouragement in excess and waste, or conflict over cultural, educational or travel matters.

SATURN shows the sense of responsibility, duty and durability of a relationship. If there is a sense of being stifled or suppressed by one's partner, it is likely that Saturn is placed in a difficult angular relationship with a personal planet in the chart of the stifled person. (The 'personal' planets are: Sun, Moon, Mercury, Venus and Mars. The other planets, Jupiter, Saturn, Uranus, Neptune and Pluto, are considered 'collective' influences.) If there is a smooth interchange of Saturnian energies with other planets, the partnership will endure more positively, with the two individuals learning a great deal about loyalty and stability from the relationship.

URANUS is famous — or notorious — for creating sudden and intense attractions which often, but not always, end as quickly as they began. Nevertheless, they are frequently as exciting and stimulating as Saturn relationships are steady and stable. However, if a Uranian type of relationship is forced into a conservative pattern, it may not endure. This is because such relationships often begin when those involved are seeking a freer type of relationship — which ends when the Uranus influence passes, or because one or both partners do not allow the other the full freedom that strong Uranus contacts between charts demands.

NEPTUNE brings to a relationship a strong sense of idealism. It makes both people more sensitive to the other's more romantic, subtle or spiritual characteristics. But it can also weave spells of illusion and make it impossible for each to see the other as he or she really is. Sometimes one individual is weak, sick, or prone to escapism through drugs, alcohol or some other illusory mechanism, and the partner feels the need to 'save' that person from themselves. Strong Neptunian relationships become highly idealised, platonic, or else are tinged with martyrdom and confusion and end up with one partner becoming disappointed and disillusioned.

PLUTO can cause two people to smother each other because of the powerful obsessive need to possess and merge totally with each other. If you are feeling overwhelmed or manipulated by your partner a strong Pluto contact between your charts may be the cause. Plutonian contacts can cause people to drag each other down or, on the positive side, to constantly renew each other and the relationship on ever higher levels.

CONCLUSION   Many astrologers, clairvoyants and the like, take it upon themselves to decide whether or not two people are suited to one another. Admittedly, they usually do so at the request of one or both parties. And, to be fair, from the point of view of harmony and compatibility they are very often correct.

It is natural for an astrologer to want to protect his or her client from unnecessary pain when it is obvious from the indications in the horoscopes that there is a strong possibility of a negative outcome and he or she can see that one or both people are going to be manipulated, oppressed, or taken advantage of. However, in trying to help such a situation, the astrologer may in fact simply be interfering, because their help may prevent someone from learning through experience. Often, when on logical analysis a relationship looks hopeless, the people in it may actually be learning exactly what they need at that time. It may well be precisely what their inner selves are driving them to experience — which has nothing at all to do with enjoyment and harmony. Although that may in fact be a part of the experience, often it can be quite the opposite.

An astrologer may see in the horoscopes that the relationship is holding one or both partners back in some way, and advise accordingly against proceeding with it. But perhaps being held back is what is needed at that time; or perhaps the individual(s) need to learn how to overcome being held back. The astrologer's role should be merely to point out the condition, not to advise an end to a relationship. When each person has learned what needs to be learned, they will end the relationship themselves.

In fact, being told that a relationship is unsuitable usually puts both parties on the defensive and they tend to ignore the advice. When in the middle of an intense relationship, however uncomfortable and stormy it is, a directive from an outsider to end it will have no effect at the emotional level. If a relationship must end, then the time must be right, that is, when one or both parties feel they are ready psychologically and emotionally to put an end to it. Or else when circumstances end it for them. Otherwise, they will simply fall into a similar situation with another partner. Even when someone leaves a situation of their own volition, they are often drawn by the same irresistible pull to another person suspiciously like the last. Habits can be broken, however compelling they may be, and how can any astrologer know whether the conditions within your relationship are not about to bring to the surface a new and enlightening knowledge about yourself? Perhaps even a knowledge that will release you from binding, outworn emotional or mental patterns.

With regard to relationship compatibility, the question is not so much whether, or even what, the astrologer should be advising. It is more important that he or she help flush out what it is within that causes us to perpetuate the negative patterns so that we can attempt to change them.

With this in mind I suggest that no one ever allow themselves to be talked into believing that their relationship cannot work. As already pointed out, an astrologer cannot know exactly what each person's needs are at a given moment, even though he or she may be able to glean a general idea. Nor can the astrologer say who is or is not 'good' for someone as far as that person's evolution or emotional development is concerned. The average astrologer is not a trained psychologist and it is highly unlikely that he or she can 'cure' any deep-seated problems. However, the astrologer can offer a clue to the causes of problems in a relationship and whether or not to act on that information is then up to the individuals concerned. Remember that whatever the stars say about your relationships (or whatever the astrologer says the stars say), their fate or success is ultimately in your own hands.

MEDICAL ASTROLOGY

This is an area where traditional astrology has a firm footing, although many relatively newly discovered glandular functions and hormones have only recently been assigned planetary and sign rulerships, over which there is some dispute. Also, medical science is constantly making discoveries, which astrology has yet to incorporate.

The foundations of medical astrology were laid in early history

— probably by Paracelsus, the Swiss–German physician and alchemist — but most certainly substantially contributed to by many other dedicated men during the course of history. One of these men was Hippocrates, whom we know as the father of modern medicine.

Many 'natural healers' use astrology in their diagnostic methods. However, they do so loosely, often using only Sun sign, Moon sign and/or Ascendant, and then only if the patient happens to know these. No doubt this additional information is useful to them, and it must be said that the field of medical astrology is a specialist field which requires as much study and experience as any other and this is possibly why most healers do not include its use more comprehensively.

Medical astrology may assist in the following areas:

DIET AND VITAMINS   The astrologer needs to have sound knowledge of basic dietary and vitamin requirements as well as the astrological correspondences. However, there are some concordances that need only a basic knowledge.

For example, many astrologers know that vitamin C is ruled by the planet Saturn, and that when Saturn in transit makes a stressful aspect to the Sun, Moon, Mercury, Venus or Mars in a natal horoscope, the traditional prognosis would be the possibility of a common cold. If the astrologer knows these relationships, he or she can recommend an increase of vitamin C in the diet during the period in which the tendency is indicated.

The planet Mars is thought to rule vitamin B_{12}, which is often absent in the diet of vegetarians. If Mars in the natal chart is under stress, either through transit or indicated in the natal horoscope as an innate tendency to be deficient in this vitamin, the astrologer might recommend an extra intake of this substance, either in tablet form or through foods with a high content of B_{12}.

All the planets and signs have vitamin and dietary correspondences and it could be useful for us to know which foods and vitamins we might innately be more in need of to attain optimum good health.

FERTILITY CYCLES AND BIRTH CONTROL   These areas are controversial in the field of astrological research, where some astounding claims have been made with regard to the accuracy of astrologically planned conception and birth control — particularly the former. These methods are based on the relationship between the Sun and Moon in a woman's natal horoscope. For her, the most fertile period during the month is said to be when the Moon returns to the same relationship that it had with the Sun during the time of her birth. If this coincides with the accepted period of fertility at ovulation, then — it is claimed — conception is practically guaranteed. On the other hand, this same method should, theoretically, be useful for birth control.

Unfortunately, it may not be as simple as it first appears, and this is where the controversy arises. The Moon does indeed return every month to the same relationship it had with the Sun in the natal chart. However, the more finical astrologers point out that the Moon in fact only returns to this *exact* relationship when it is in the same 'declination' as well — that is, in the same position north or south of the Moon's path around the Earth, as well as in the same longitude. This does not happen nearly so often. Others claim that their research proves this latter disparity to be irrelevant.

Those seeking to conceive would not lose anything by consulting an astrologer for these most favourable times — and it only takes a few minutes to work them out once the astrologer has constructed the birth chart and knows exactly where the Moon is. However, I doubt that too many astrologers would guarantee, or even advocate, the use of this system alone for birth control purposes.

CHOOSING THE BABY'S GENDER   This is another claim that does not yet seem to have been verified with any firm data, even though its supposedly high level of accuracy is widely recognised and accepted in astrological circles. This is how it is done:

Conceive the child on a day when the Moon is in a sign

that accords with the preferred sex. That is, when the Moon is in a 'positive' or masculine sign such as Aries, Gemini, Leo, Libra, Sagittarius or Aquarius, it is theoretically possible to conceive a boy child. When the Moon is in a 'negative' or feminine sign such as Taurus, Cancer, Virgo, Scorpio, Capricorn or Pisces, one should be able to conceive a girl child.

The difficulties here are that conception does not always take place immediately, and that, unless you understand the workings of the ephemeris or tables of planetary positions, you will not know where the Moon is.

If it were possible to control the child's gender in this manner, it might raise an objection on the grounds of bio-ecological imbalance. However, since its accuracy is questionable, anyone who feels like testing the theory should go right ahead!

ELECTIVE SURGERY   Traditional astrology has a single dominating rule with regard to the undergoing of surgical operations: no operation should take place when the Moon is in the sign that rules the part of the body on which the operation is to be performed. The suggestion is that you should wait until it has moved into another sign.

For example, if the part of the body to be operated on is the knee, surgery should be avoided when the Moon is passing through Capricorn, and so on through all the signs and their physiological correspondences, which any astrologer can supply. This is particularly applicable if the Moon receives unfavourable aspects from other planets as it is passing through the relevant sign — especially from (or to) Mars, which rules incisions, surgeons and also damage.

Naturally, emergency operations cannot be planned around this rule and, again, the overall astrological picture has to be taken into consideration.

As a matter of interest, I underwent an appendectomy when the Moon was in Aries, which is Mars' sign, thus violating the second rule concerning surgical operations: no operation should take place when the Moon is in the signs ruling incisions (Aries or Scorpio), or in stressful aspect to Mars. Whether it had anything to do with the fact that this rule was not obeyed I do not know, but complications followed and recovery was slow. However, even had I known anything about astrology at the time, the urgency and suddenness of the condition would certainly not have allowed me to stay the surgeon's hand with a plea to 'wait till the Moon leaves Aries!'

But, with many types of operations one does have a choice and if there is a possibility of enhancing recovery in any way, there would seem to be no harm in avoiding a time that might be less propitious.

DIAGNOSIS   Medical astrology can be a boon in assisting diagnosis. This is, I feel, the best use to which medical astrology can be put. It is also a valuable tool in pinpointing potential physical weaknesses which could lead to problems in the future. Such knowledge can help us to strengthen and protect those areas.

Conversely, there is a potentially major hazard if astrological diagnosis is used carelessly and we allow ourselves to give in to negative suggestion.

The subject of human suggestibility is becoming a specialised field of research in its own right. In the area of cancer research, for instance, there are certain schools of thought that believe the high rate of mortality due to cancer is in some way connected with the patient's belief — as well as all those around him or her, including the attending doctor — that death from this disease is virtually inevitable. Such is the power of suggestion. Unfortunately, many astrologers are completely oblivious to an individual's degree of suggestibility — which has nothing to do with a client's apparent response, which may well appear favourable. Consequently, you should try to be aware of your own real susceptibility and treat with caution any health diagnosis given to you by an astrologer.

Those astrologers who have any commonsense at all do not indulge in irresponsible speculation about death. But many seemingly sensible practitioners still have a tendency to speculate about illness *per se*, which is no less detrimental to one's sense of well-being and faith in the future. If an astrologer makes any unsolicited, particularly negative, predictions about your health that you find unnerving, seek the advice of another astrologer who will look at the situation less sensationally. Serious illness is impossible to diagnose in a straightforward manner from the horoscope alone because there is a multitude of variables to consider. It needs a considerable knowledge of anatomy and physiology, as well as the aetiology of disease, along with a thorough grounding in medical astrology, to be an expert in this field.

However, as mentioned, an astrologer can provide useful hints about taking precautionary measures during low- or high-energy periods. If the astrologer is well-versed in the subject, he or she might be able to advise someone who is astrologically indicated as being prone to stomach or liver disorders, for example, to make sure they get plenty of fresh air, eat fresh and wholesome foods, and refrain from overindulgence in rich or greasy foods.

Even though this sort of advice is simple commonsense, a warning might be warranted if the astrologer sees in the offing an increase in a person's susceptibility in their weak area. It is also about the upper limit to any medical advice given by an astrologer who is not a doctor and/or a specialist in this field. So, if you are consulting an astrologer primarily for the purpose of diagnosis of health problems, make your choice with great care, preferably only on the recommendation of someone whom you trust, and in conjunction with professional medical advice.

Astrology can, without doubt, be a valuable diagnostic aid, especially with illnesses that defy the more usual methods of diagnosis. An astrologer might just be able to suggest some new angle that has perhaps been overlooked or not considered, or new areas that could be examined by your doctor. The drawback to this, of course, is that there are few doctors who are open-minded enough to accept the possibility that astrology may have something constructive to offer in this field. But there is hope, for attitudes are slowly changing. I have witnessed the positive application of sound advice in instances where potentially nasty illnesses were forestalled with astrological diagnosis. However, I have also witnessed many cases where nothing eventuated from indications of potential health breakdowns.

My advice is: do not accept any single astrologer's word as final in health matters and do not be tempted to try to cure yourself on astrological advice. This is especially true if you are under a doctor's care for a serious illness.

It should be clear by now that medical astrology is a highly complex field, requiring more than even a prolific knowledge of astrology to accurately diagnose an illness. Responsible astrologers would *never* prescribe a remedy, except perhaps herbal or vitamin supplements, light exercise, and so on. Even medical practitioners have trouble prescribing correctly sometimes, and medicine is their specialised field.

If you do wish to consult an astrologer on a serious medical question, I repeat, go only to one who is recommended, or who is recognised as a thoroughly competent medical astrologer. And seek professional medical advice both before and after the consultation.

RELOCATION

Many astrologers believe that if one is going to relocate, one should move to a place that blends harmoniously or profitably with one's natal horoscope. I feel this is somewhat impracticable. The impetus to relocate usually results from finding a place where one would rather be and rarely from a desire simply to change one's address. I have never heard of anyone who benefited from having approached the matter from this latter angle, although it is possible to do this — and we will examine this situation shortly.

However, I can certainly see the benefits to be gained from understanding how a proposed move is likely to affect one.

What happens in a horoscope when a person moves to another location — if the move is distant enough — is an alteration in emphasis within the natal chart. This comes about through the house cusps changing their positions, which in turn alters the avenues through which the planetary energies are directed. This means that some areas of personal experience and expression are emphasised and require closer attention than before, while other areas are de-emphasised.

It must be remembered that relocating will not change the basic tone of the chart. The fundamental character and needs will remain the same. The difference lies only in the circumstantial opportunity for expressing these fundamental characteristics.

As mentioned, it is theoretically possible to consult an astrologer about choosing an area or town that might more profitably release certain trapped energies or alter the focus of one's life if desired.

Suppose, for example, you wished to move to a location where better job opportunities might exist. The astrologer would look for a city in a geographical position in which a chart set up for these new coordinates would move your natal Sun, Saturn, or any other personal career indicators, to a more prominent position in the horoscope. Such a move could not be guaranteed to transform suddenly your professional image and status, of course. This would depend upon other considerations, including your own skills and capacities.

As an illustration, a client uprooted himself and moved to another country in a different hemisphere. A chart set up for the new location — after the event — was found to correlate accurately in every way with his experiences. The cusp of the house which represented Career in the chart moved from the sign of Sagittarius (he worked in publishing, with which Sagittarius is connected) to Capricorn. This sign can signify extra responsibilities or difficulties with the profession. As it turned out, his professional reputation suffered. Furthermore, Saturn (which rules Capricorn) moved to an area of the chart that is connected with the finances. Adding these together it might have signified having to work harder or working for less money. In this instance it resulted in severe restrictions to his finances.

Still other indications in the relocation chart were of changes in health, and marital upheavals — both of which occurred.

These results did not have to work out this way. They were dependent on other issues, such as his psychological state, his physical condition and his financial state at the time. These matters would also have been aggravated by current transits and progressions, and so on. In other words, it was only possible for his potential at that time to be fulfilled. The same relocation at another period of his life would probably have resulted in a completely different outcome, because of such changes as a more mature outlook or different work.

In the midst of worrying and wondering whether illness or poverty will strike in a new location, one should not overlook the *meaning* of these external manifestations of trouble. It is likely that the actual purpose of moving, as well as the degree of one's psychological awareness, would contribute greatly to, perhaps even determine, the conditions that arise. If, for instance, an individual has not yet developed a mature attitude to financial management, and the area in the chart that represents values comes under stress, it is almost certainly going to mean problems with money and possessions. And if this person has not yet learned to deal with his or her responsibilities, then there will very likely be some effect on the health, because both these matters are related to the same area of the chart (the 6th house).

There are other methods of assessing a relocation. A horary chart (see pages 94–5) can be erected for the time when the idea of moving occurs, or for the time one arrives at a new location. In fact, if you wish to take advantage of *all* the methods available for this exercise you could have an astrologer erect a horary chart, an electional chart, a relocation chart and a comparison between your own horoscope and that of the place you wish to move to. You could then have him or her check the current transits and progressions to your own chart! But if you attempt all this you are asking for trouble because there is one rule in astrology, which applies to all divinatory art, and that is, ask only once, and ask clearly. Otherwise you will be more confused than if you had not asked at all. A simple relocation chart should be sufficient to provide a lot of insight into any proposed change of locale.

MUNDANE ASTROLOGY
There are several categories that fall under this heading. Few would be of concern to the layman, who would generally not feel the necessity to consult an astrologer about such subjects. But in case you do not realise that an astrologer can be consulted on these issues, they are included here.

WEATHER PREDICTION AND NATURAL DISASTERS

This is a specialised field, the basic principles for which were established in the very early days of astrology and related to the various 'humours' of the planets. For example, the 'humour' of the Sun is, as would be expected, hot and dry, Saturn is cold and dry, Venus cool and wet, and so on. These humours are modified according to the position of the planet, the aspects other planets make to it, and the sign it occupies in the chart drawn up for the place in question.

Although I have seen a better rate of accuracy from astrological weather prediction than I have from meteorological forecasts, I would not plan a camping holiday by it.

Major catastrophes like cyclones, tornadoes, earthquakes and volcanic eruptions are predictable. However, this, regrettably, is another area where astrologers are renowned for their hindsight. This is because it is well nigh impossible to pinpoint such events beforehand, among the multitude of shifting planetary relationships which combine briefly to create the precise patterns representing such major upheavals.

In this realm, it is science rather than astrology that seems to be making significant progress with the understanding of planetary relationships and their correspondence with natural disasters.

POLITICS AND ECONOMICS

Political and economical predictions are frequent and, in my opinion, among the bravest, or most foolish, forecasting attempted by astrologers. Since these two subjects were among the earliest practised by astrologers, they should, theoretically, boast the highest rate of accuracy. But that is not the case. Nonetheless, despite the number of failures astrologers have in these fields, many still dream of the day when they will publicly broadcast a major event that will come to pass as predicted. Whether it is a worldwide economic recession or the Apocalypse is irrelevant, what matters is that they will at last be believed — even if it is only at the moment of extinction!

To astrologers, catastrophes are perennially fascinating. But if they wish to be more accurate they should try to be more open to the rapidly growing knowledge of astronomers and other scientists, who seem to be closer to understanding which planetary or cosmic events or relationships 'cause', or are connected with, major earthly ones.

The patterns of our skies are like a kaleidoscope of ever-changing designs, each moment creating new compositions that reflect sometimes subtle, sometimes distinct and radical qualities and events on our tiny planet near the edge of our galaxy.

It is, and probably will be for some time to come, more a matter of chance or accident when an astrologer forecasts such events — any events — precisely. There are, after all, so many forces at work in the universe that the day is yet to arrive when humanity not only knows what they all are but also how to interpret them correctly.

ⓂSPIRITUAL QUESTIONS

Although many astrologers are being influenced by mythology and its psychological roots, there are still a great many whose standpoints are based on the Theosophical tradition and its Eastern philosophies and religious ideologies. Such astrologers believe in the idea of reincarnation and the laws of *karma* and *dharma* which are connected with this concept. Their interpretations of a horoscope are based on these laws.

For those who are not familiar with these terms, *dharma* is the 'law of being', of 'right living', which means living according to one's higher nature. This is one of astrology's most fundamental canons, for its main aim has long been to help all human beings to discover how they can live their lives according to their best qualities, thereby furthering their spiritual evolution.

Karma is considered to be the great equaliser. It is the 'debts to be paid' for past actions. Relationships, particularly, are assessed on the basis of this theme. It is believed that how we act always has either a good or bad effect on others, to the extent that we meet up in future lives, again and again, with those to whom we are in debt (or they to us) until such a debt is fully discharged.

There are astrologers who are strongly influenced by these ideas and who are positive and constructive in their interpretations. Their view is that astrology can help us understand what these 'karmic retributions' are, where they come from, how they are affecting us, and how we can make recompense — 'balance the scales of justice' — as expeditiously as possible. If you believe strongly in such precepts, you may well find solace in this type of interpretation.

However, certain astrologers are overly zealous about the idea of *karma* and dole out pessimism and hopelessness under the guise of spiritual advice: 'You can't do anything about it; it's your karma and you just have to accept it . . . ' is a favourite, irrespective of whether they are advising on a person's state of health, a relationship or a set of circumstances. It is an easy way out and is sometimes done simply for effect. If this is the kind of advice you get, and given that the astrologer is not a god, it might be safer and more fruitful to find an astrologer who prefers to examine *with you* what has occurred in your present life that draws you to repeat negative experiences, rather than one who makes unverifiable allusions to what you did to deserve such 'bad *karma*' in some dubious previous existence.

Whatever each of us needs in the area of spirituality, it is obviously highly personal and requires an extremely sensitive touch. It is difficult enough for anyone to know their own spiritual truths without misguiding others. So if you want to know what your *dharma* and/or *karma* is by astrological means, please use discretion.

CRISES

The psychological rule says that when an inner situation is not made conscious, it happens outside as fate. That is to say, when the individual remains undivided and does not become conscious of his inner contradictions, the world must perforce act out the conflict and be torn into opposite halves.

C. G. JUNG, THE COLLECTED WORKS, VOL. 9. PART II, 'AION'.

Crises can occur at any time in our lives but many major turning points coincide with astrologically notable planetary configurations which happen to all of us around the same age.

Many of these periods coincide with what is referred to as the Saturn Cycle. Saturn takes approximately 28 years to orbit the

Sun, and every seven (that magic number!) years it makes a powerful aspect to its original position in the natal horoscope. Often, these Saturn periods correspond with other planetary cycles and we unwittingly refer to those ages with the key words associated with the planets concerned.

For instance, at the age of 21, Saturn is in a strong, harmonious relationship with its natal position. Saturn is connected with responsibility and duty. At this age, too, Uranus is similarly in strong aspect to its natal position, except it is a more dynamic angle, which makes it sharper, and our personal reaction to its influence more rebellious and independent. Uranus is connected with individualisation. So, we hand to our 21-year-olds the 'key to the door', which is the symbol of our recognition of their having attained an age when they are, theoretically, *responsible* (which is the Saturnian key word) enough to deserve the *freedom* to be *independent* (both Uranian key words).

Between the ages of 27 and 30, Saturn returns to its original place in the personal horoscope. So often our best choices come after this first Saturn Return, as it is called, and which is in many ways a 'rebirth'. During this time we are forced to reassess who we are and where we really fit into the grand scheme of life. This period is especially significant because Saturn has by now passed through every sign and house within the natal chart. Saturn represents the material world, so having touched every area by the age of 30, it has made everything in our world 'real' to us. It has introduced to our conscious awareness every phase of worldly experience — insofar as we are capable of absorbing it and to the extent that our circumstances permit.

Saturn also defines our personal boundaries. This means that by the time it has traversed every segment and planet in the chart it has given us an idea of our limitations — or what we think are our limitations, although we may later transcend them.

Usually during this period we feel a strong need to establish ourselves concretely in our world, or at least to reorientate our lives in a direction that will give us the same effect. It is very much a time to take stock of who we really are, for it is the beginning of a new 28-year cycle where we should re-experience every one of those areas of life on a higher, that is, more aware, level. Now we should begin to know that we are unique and must find our place in the world. Now we must realise we are no longer duplicates of our parents or peers and that it is time for us to establish our own selves and re-evaluate the roles we choose to fill. Even if we continue along the same path, some new facet of that path will present itself and demand to be dealt with to show us the same realisations.

Sometimes the transition to this new self may take place relatively effortlessly. Sometimes it takes a crisis — or several — to force us to wake up to our newly developing identities. Sometimes we ignore the promptings altogether and our lives remain stagnant, which will inevitably create difficulties at some stage in the future when we are finally forced to recognise those needs via some external upheaval. The longer we resist taking any necessary steps to do what we should do in this respect — and be who we should be — the less we will be able to cope with the way in which those unrecognised needs outwardly manifest themselves.

The next period of major transition occurs in our late thirties to early forties. Just when we think we have it all worked out, the powerful, inexorable outer planets all join forces again to jolt us out of the complacence we may have settled into. During this time there is often a growing feeling that life has become meaningless and that the years have been wasted. In a desperate attempt to find meaning, or to quench an undefinable craving, people often completely upset their lives and leave spouse and family, job, home, perhaps even country.

If any of these responses are in answer to the true inner call, then it will very possibly result in a new lease on life, and then life really 'begins at 40'. However, it is not always a positive response because it is the inner self that must be allowed freedom of expression and merely changing the environment is not always sufficient. It is even less so if one tries to retain outworn values.

The new self can often be just as well expressed in the same, or similar, mode of existence as before, simply by changing one's attitude in general. Sometimes, it must be admitted, the outer and old style of life can no longer be supported and change in some form frequently follows because it is necessary.

There is really only one way to deal with life during such times and that is consciously and purposely to seek out exactly what true independence and freedom mean *personally*. If you are the one to whom all the 'bad luck' seems to be happening, it is no use blaming others or bemoaning your lot in life. You can be sure that in some way life is telling you to look into yourself and find out who is really there. It is time to step forward bravely into your future without a backward glance or a single regret. If you do, life is more likely to open up for you. If you do not, you may drown in your own self-pity for as long as it takes to wake up to yourself.

'Self-pity' is one of the key words of Neptune — a planet that complicates the experiences of this period between 40 and 42. This is because, while Uranus is urging towards further individualisation and independence, Neptune seems to be acting to accomplish the opposite: to dissolve one's sense of identity and uniqueness.

Neptune's task is to merge the individual into the common pool of humanity, to show us where we are like everyone else underneath our surface separateness. This can lead to tolerance and compassion for one's fellow creatures, for one is able to identify with, and understand, humanity's pain, tragedy — or beauty — depending on the level of one's realisation. On the other hand, it can fill one with panic and confusion at the threat this can carry, particularly as this is also the threshold of middle age and the future no longer seems to stretch out endlessly.

However, although these two planets appear to be working against each other, they can in fact combine to give a sense of uniqueness, yet also of belonging. Neptune dissolves any sense of separateness from the rest of life, or of the world, caused by the ego. Saturn joins in the 'attack' too at this time, so that the outcome can be that a concrete individuality (Uranus) is re-established (Saturn) which is not dependent upon the ego-structure that is being attacked but upon something more solid and deeper within.

Often these pressures create a period of confusion about one's goals, purpose and identity. For a man whose life has usually been spent in aiming for specific goals and fulfilling certain ambitions, such doubts can be completely disorienting. For a woman, the difficulty often focuses on her role as mother, for her children may now be growing up and becoming more independent, leaving her with an increasing sense of uselessness. Then, of course, there are the physiological changes, which can be a challenge in their own right — particularly for a woman, who can now see menopause on the horizon and wrinkles and sagging in the mirror, while her husband may be looking more 'distinguished' and 'experienced' rather than simply 'old'.

Most succumb to the confusion, self-doubt and lack of direction at this time, which occurs to varying degrees and for differing periods. The man who is struggling to fulfil someone else's goals (his parents', society's, etc.), or even his own if they are for superficial reasons, is bound to feel momentarily lost when he is confronted with the thought that they are meaningless and that, therefore, so is his life. The woman who defines her sense of self by her children's dependence upon her will be shattered when those children begin to reach out to the world instead of only to her.

This is a time when many people end up in the offices of the doctor, psychologist, and other counsellors — all of whom can give guidance and support through the difficult cycle. However, the astrologer has the advantage of having access to information that the client cannot tell to other counsellors — mainly because he or she does not know it, being caught up in the immediate situation. The astrologer can see instantly the type of energies and areas affecting and being affected by current issues and feelings. He or she can also get a fair idea of the time span of each influence and what it might lead into next; in the meantime constructively guiding people through their crises to the point where they can begin anew. And this is where Pluto comes into the picture.

Pluto's principle is regeneration — which can occur only after the outworn and obsolete conditions, or modes of operation, have been annihilated. In the psyche, Pluto achieves this by plumbing the depths and forcing hidden and destructive qualities, attitudes, ideas and feelings, to the surface to be eliminated; those ways of thinking, acting and being that are no longer relevant to the new form that is developing, and which become poison to the psyche.

Pluto highlights the personal part one plays within the social whole by creating a confrontation with social conditions. For example, those born when Pluto was passing through the sign of Cancer (1912–38) experienced a shaking of their very foundations (as a group) when Pluto transited the sign of Libra (1971–84). Their fundamental attitudes towards home life and the family unit (Cancerian matters) were challenged at a very deep level by the world movement towards upheaval of the institution of marriage (a Libran matter). This movement undermined the basic structure of the home and family.

Pluto therefore gets at the roots of the masses and pulls them up in order to make room for new strains, new ideas, new forms. Old laws (Libra) were challenged and a new type of co-operation (also a Libra function) had to be learned if those changes were to be adapted to and used constructively. We will continue to see this particular effect for years to come as we gradually adjust to a different concept and arrangement of 'family'.

Those born when Pluto was in Leo (1938–57) will experience social change and upheaval when Pluto passes through the sign of Scorpio (its own sign and therefore highly potent in its effects here) between 1984 and 1995. This generation's will to dominate, and the power plays in their efforts to do so, will meet their nemesis in a worldwide Scorpionic purge of ego-oriented megalomaniacs. There are indications that this is already happening.

There has been much conjecture about Pluto's transit through its own sign, particularly as it crosses inside Neptune's orbit and is the closest it has ever been to the Sun. Some suggest major medical breakthroughs and discoveries, others say it will be annihilation and regeneration of our resources, both economic and ecological. Others say it will be Armageddon ... but then someone always does!

Whatever eventuates, it will be the generation of individuals born with Pluto in Leo who will have the most significant hand in affairs as power plays become all-consuming and everyone wants to lead. These people will also be the most personally affected — at least as far as their collective root structure is concerned. This does not mean that those born with Pluto in other signs would not be affected or experience any changes. It means that they would not experience them in such a potentially personally transforming way. Those born with Pluto in Cancer for example, came from a background of family solidity and stability which had formed during the course of many centuries. This was changed drastically during their lifetime by two world wars and the Depression. Family stability was undermined by these disasters and it was that generation of mothers who began the back-to-work-at-40 movement, because the old patterns no longer worked or offered refuge.

Those born earlier, with Pluto in Gemini, would have been less affected by these particular problems because their family structure was threatened *after* they had left the safety of their own childhood and gone out into the world. Those born later, with Pluto in Leo, were also affected by the changes initiated before they were born. But because they were born *into* those changes, their roots were already in a different social and familial structure. Consequently, they too would not be affected in the same way as the Pluto in Cancer generation.

The Pluto confrontation also occurs in the early forties age-group — at least during the latter portion of this century, owing to this planet's faster speed. People born at the turn of the century did not experience this Pluto confrontation until they were in their sixties, and the same will apply to those born well into the twenty-first century. We are the dubiously lucky recipients of getting all the major pressures associated with the slow-moving planets around the same period in our lives. In one respect this should force us to evolve and grow that much faster because it is more intense. Also, I suppose you could say we get it over with in one go. But it also results in more broken marriages (and therefore possibly more insecure children), and more illness as a result of the intense and long, drawn-out pressures. There is also much more confusion and unhappiness at a personal level. All of this is our sacrifice for the long-term collective benefit.

The next major stage in an individual's development occurs around the ages of 56 to 59 when a new period of reorientation is beginning. This superficially represents an adjustment to the idea of approaching 'old age', and underneath there should be a culmination to true maturity — at least for those who have been able to utilise opportunities and adjust to the passage of time in a constructive and positive way. This is the second 'Saturn Return' of our lives and, yet again, metaphorically a third birth, with all the possibilities of beginning again, once more at a higher and greater level of awareness.

Further culminations occur around the age of 70, and again at 84. This latter age marks a major astrological milestone, even apart from the obvious victory of having travelled so far through time. At the age of 84, Uranus — planet of individualisation — has completed *one* journey through the full zodiac, suggesting that at this age a human being has potentially fully developed his or her full uniqueness.

The crises we go through periodically, which seem so often like cruel injustices or else pointless self-torture, and which our rational minds, or even our friends and relatives, might tell us to snap out of, are obviously more than passing phases in most cases. They are often major transitions to a new and greater self. As such, those times, and people going through them, should be treated with utmost respect, for each or any of them has the power to make an individual a slave to their past or a master of their present.

2 PITFALLS AND MISUSES

When the astrologer and client first come together, they are meeting under the cumulative effect of many influences: heredity, environment and the weight of astrology's past, to name a few. These will inevitably contaminate their interchange. It will affect their personal perceptions of what an astrologer is: their expectations, presumptions, and hopes. As this will colour how the astrologer approaches the client, and how the client responds, certain problems may arise which forewarning may help to avoid.

THE PITFALLS OF BEING TOO BELIEVING

If you visit an astrologer in the middle of a crisis, as most people do, you will probably be feeling some degree of insecurity and self-doubt. You will be more vulnerable than usual to persuasion or suggestion, and reluctant to take an initiative in your life. Consequently, you may want the astrologer to relieve you of your worries by making your decisions for you. If this is the way you feel — *beware*, for not all astrologers are pure of heart and even those who are can have basic human failings.

To avoid wasting your time and money — which are precious enough — but mainly to avoid being misguided, you should be aware of what you are really asking for. And also what the astrologer is really trying to give you.

Those astrologers of the more humane variety could be pressured by your helplessness and need into telling you what you want to hear: prophesying a future that makes you feel better rather than guiding you gently and constructively towards the reality. This may provide a temporary relief but it is not going to help in the long term. In fact, when the reality occurs, its unexpectedness, coupled with your disillusionment with the astrologer whom you trusted, will make it even harder to take.

There are less humane astrologers too, and these people may be inexperienced, irresponsible or unprincipled — yet impressive enough to create a sense of trust, even awe, which they thrive on. If you are easily duped by apparent expertise or showmanship, whether it is your natural tendency or the result of being under strain, you are easy prey.

All astrologers, not just the charlatans, run the risk, as much as psychologists, doctors, or any experts, of being automatically accepted as supreme authorities in their fields. Whether for their egos, or for your own good (at least as they see it), they are bound to try to put you on the 'right path'. Naturally, this will veer towards their ideas of what 'right' is, and in the process they may try to impose on you their own moral codes, religious beliefs and a host of other personal biases. Even those who have no such intentions and are of good intent can get trapped into doing this by the expectations placed on them in their roles as counsellors. They can forget that your will to choose may be undermined by their efforts to guide you, which at times can come very close to converting others to their way of thinking.

What astrology can and should do, is reinforce our confidence to make our own decisions, whether those decisions are the right or wrong ones. At least then we will be on our own paths and not someone else's.

Obviously, the astrologer's subjective view is bound to affect his or her interpretation to some extent, and this is not always negative. It is in fact what makes each astrologer's style uniquely appropriate to each individual's needs. The crucial issue is to discriminate between what is purely professional advice and what is only personal opinion.

As a suggested guideline, the professional advice of an astrologer should ideally be limited to describing or defining your character, or situation. This should allow *you* to decide for yourself what you accept as true and relevant, and what action you will take, if any. Within their professional scope, astrologers can also offer alternatives of action according to what they see indicated in your horoscope at the time.

The decision of how much, and whether or not to take advice based on another person's private opinions is, of course, finally your own. If you genuinely want someone else's personal views, then I suggest that the safest approach is to use the astrologer as a sounding board. Bounce your thoughts, feelings and experiences off them to help you get a wider perspective. However, please do not rely on an astrologer to solve your problems for you. And, most of all, do not let any moral judgments they may make affect your actions and decisions against your own real wishes and instincts.

If you choose an astrologer who is sincere, responsible and capable, remember that no quality, however admirable or endearing, is going to guarantee accuracy, either about your character, or in the prediction of your future circumstances.

There are many instances of spectacular accuracy in astrology's history, but these seem to be confined mainly to a time when individuals and societies were more restricted by racial and geographical limitations, class, dogma and rules of conduct.

Through scientific, technological and psychological advances, our lives have become much more complicated, greatly increasing the number of possible pathways to Fate. It would, therefore, be logical if accuracy in the prediction of which paths we will take at any particular moment has decreased proportionately.

The subject of astrology itself has become increasingly complex due to these developments. With the introduction of the computer into this field, we are being supplied with an endless stream of innovative and sophisticated techniques. Astronomy, physics, math and psychology are also bombarding us with a steady flow of new information, all of which has to be tested and integrated into the main body of astrology before it can be put into practice with any reliability. The psychological depths alone, into which astrology can now penetrate, bear no resemblance to the comparatively superficial inquiry into human nature carried on for so many centuries. Similarly, the extent of our physiological knowledge enables us to use astrology in medical areas far more comprehensively than ever anticipated by such astro-medical titans as Paracelsus.

There may be numerous other reasons why astrological prediction is frequently unreliable. But whatever the reasons, there is one maxim each person should take with them to their astrological interview: astrological predictions should never be accepted as immutable laws. They are not fates ... *not ever*.

To reinforce this warning, the following are a few real-life reasons to remember that maxim.

In my early astrological days, when I was what you could call a starry-eyed neophyte, I had the first hefty jolt to my faith in astrological forecasting. I had studied just enough of the subject to know that planetary influences shortly to affect my horoscope were traditionally regarded as 'life-threatening'.

To be honest, I was more than slightly concerned. So, I asked my astrology teacher what he thought might happen to me when the influence was due, hoping he would allay my fears and reassure me. Since he was my astrological superior I accepted his word unquestioningly. Consequently, when he told me that I might be the victim of an act of violence, I was duly horrified. Shamelessly, to impress his gullible student further, he offered me the alternative: that I myself might do violence to someone else!

As it happened, I was in India during the time the 'disaster' was supposed to occur. It was my first visit and I had been well primed by many a traveller's gory tale about that country. And I could not, however hard I tried, ignore the fears that had so sensationally been implanted in my impressionable mind.

Fortunately, I met an astrologer who had a much broader view of the subject and he managed to assuage my worst fears so that I could at least try to enjoy the rest of my Indian adventure. Nonetheless, the seed had been planted and in a tiny corner of my mind I continued to be worried that something would happen. And it did. But not at all in the manner that had been suggested. The aspects themselves in fact related to the visit to India *per se*. Few could visit such a country and not be changed by it. So, in effect, the 'injury' did occur. However, what was 'damaged' was my old way of looking at life, not my body. As a result of that journey, my entire attitude towards life was broadened and deepened.

Despite the error made in the foregoing example, astrology can — in situations that are potentially dangerous — provide a useful warning to be more thoughtful in the way one conducts oneself.

I thought to take advantage of this to increase the safety factor on a bicycle tour with a friend. Riding on country roads in Australia, where giant semitrailers with mighty tail-winds charge down the narrow two-lane highways, is perilous and nervewracking. So, I checked our horoscopes. Everything seemed favourable. I was caught completely by surprise, therefore, when my friend fell off his bike, hurting himself seriously enough to put an end to the trip. And it occurred in such a perfectly innocent and ludicrous situation — just to show that astrology was right in not indicating 'great danger'!

I had slowed down to look for a place to rest. Having spotted a delightfully shady place, I pulled up. My partner, unbeknown to me, was at that moment perilously close to my rear wheel. He could not avoid hitting it. And although it was only a gentle knock, it stopped him mid-pedal. As any cyclist would know, it is easier to keep a bicycle upright when it is in motion. When stationary, it has a tendency to become parallel with the ground. And even though it did this in slow motion, my friend could not avoid joining it. He broke his arm in two places.

I could not believe it. There had been nothing in the horoscope that I could see to indicate the far-reaching effects this had on our future plans. It not only put an end to our proposed year of travel, but while restlessly waiting for the arm to heal we moved to a completely new location, which changed our lifestyle and committed us to a more settled future.

The only possible astrological indication of disruption at that moment was so minor I had ignored it. There would be a lot more broken limbs and bodies struggling around if such an accident happened whenever this aspect turned up, for it occurs in everyone's horoscopes once each month. Owing to its short duration of influence (lasting only a couple of hours) it is usually indicative of petty irritations rather than long-term effects. The type of planetary aspects that are prone to extend their effects into the future tend to last in a person's horoscope for up to a couple of years.

I do not profess to know all there is to know about astrology, and among all the complex and varied systems used in prognostication I might easily have missed some pattern indicating the event. But astrology is used by many as a reliable predictive tool, and if it is, there should have been some obvious traditional indicator to show that such a significant event was imminent. Similarly in the case of the prediction of a violent fate for me in India when no such disaster happened, there should not have been the strong indications that there were. And so on through all the other missed or miscalculated fates during the long history of astrology.

The greatest puzzle for astrologers seems to lie in selecting the level of life on which the effects are going to be played out: physical or psychological. Also, whether it will be the result of a personal action or of someone else's action. Whatever the prediction, it is clear that astrology, at least as far as our present knowledge and understanding goes, cannot *consistently* foretell specific events.

It is true that an experienced astrologer can see the possibility of financial problems, which might require a tightening of the moneybelt. And it might mean the loss of your job or a business failure. However, the same horoscope indications could just as easily mean there is something you will want to buy, or do, that requires more money, and consequently that you will have to restrain your spending and/or work harder to attain the goal.

It could also mean, for any number of reasons, that you will become more disciplined with your money and try to get by on less.

It is also possible, for those astrologers who have studied the medical aspect of the art, to see which organs or bodily systems are likely to be under duress, and when. But they cannot say that you will, without question, fall ill — unless you are so suggestible you make it come true. (I know of one astrologer who makes herself ill whenever she sees the possibility indicated in her own horoscope.)

Astrologers can also see when you, or someone around you, might make an impulsive move that could result in an accident to you. But they cannot know for sure that you will be hurt as a result, or whether it will eventuate as a quarrel, a headache, a minor breakage, or some other disruption.

The most useless prophecy is that of death. Whether it be of your own impending demise or that of someone close to you, it is impossible for the ordinary everyday astrologer, as the majority are, to astrologically predict certain death. It would take a superhuman being to manage this — and would such a being really wish or need to resort to astrology? Even the ancient astrologers, who, apparently, were superior in their knowledge and accuracy, were not able to predict death with any consistent accuracy, no more than they were able to predict any event. Moreover, any astrologer who attempts to do so has questionable motives. What possible assistance can such information give to anyone if it is unsolicited and unwanted?

Astrologers who insist on forecasting death offer the excuse that it is 'better to be prepared'. However, commonsense says that if it is possible the event will not happen at all, such a reason does not seem valid. A constant shadow hanging over the future is hardly a positive preparation and will inevitably restrict a person's aims and actions, and therefore limit their fulfilment.

If you really want to know such information, and your astrologer is willing to try to give it to you, that is your business. But to you who are given unsolicited prophecies of death, I strongly suggest you ignore them. Furthermore, I would suggest you ignore any sensationalistic doomsaying at all, for the astrologer who resorts to this is often merely indulging in theatrics.

If this happens to you, go and find an astrologer whose reputation suggests a more constructive and responsible attitude, an astrologer who will show you how a predicted failure may be turned into a success if you make the effort and who will show you equally how a promised success can fail if you sit back and wait for it to happen (because an astrologer said it would). Better still — find such an astrologer in the first place and save yourself a lot of pain and trouble.

Let me repeat: an astrologer can guide you well. But his or her word should *never* be accepted as law. Which leads me to my final warning about being too believing.

If the astrologer you consult also believes that the 'Fate' written in the stars is unalterable, this could encourage you to blame astrology for what you are and for what happens to you. Statements like 'the stars made you what you are ... it's *karma*!' are an indication of this type of attitude.

It is so easy to blame astrology because the stars and planets are impersonal bodies with seemingly transcendental powers. This idea is reinforced by each planet's being equated with a mythological deity and conferred with his or her powers, which we, as mere mortals, could not possibly hope to mitigate.

In mythology, when human beings dared to challenge the word of the gods, this act was called *hubris* and was a 'sin' punishable by the gods themselves. Well, we *are* committing *hubris* in our efforts to physically invade their territory in outer space, as well as inner space, with our challenge to the fate determined by our heredity. And our growing collective psychological upheaval could be the angry reaction of the forces within our subconscious (for the gods and planets are symbols of these internal forces), which we are stirring up with our probing and questioning.

Whether or not you should challenge the fate or inherited patterns 'decreed by the gods', or outlined by planetary signatures, is not my main concern here, however, for that is up to you.

What I am suggesting is that you challenge the astrologer's word: the human interpretation of these patterns or 'messages'. Not as a matter of course, nor just for the sake of it, but because an unquestioned acceptance, conscious or otherwise, of what the astrologer says the stars/planets/gods are saying, can undermine your will to do what you really want to do with your life and to be who you really can be. It simply takes away your courage and initiative. Which leads us full circle, for this is what superstition is all about.

Heavy warnings, all of them. But please do not be disheartened. There are many astrologers who are skilled, honest and practical. The emphasis here has been for those who are too quick to trust and too little versed in the realities of astrology and its practitioners.

If you are like this, either by nature or temporarily because of stress, all you need do is to be aware and to carry a little scepticism with you. But not too much ... because that could create another sort of problem.

☑THE PITFALLS OF BEING TOO SUSPICIOUS
There is less potential danger in being too suspicious than in being too trusting. Nonetheless, it can interfere with possible benefits.

Suspicion seems to be set off or aggravated when the astrologer asks questions, for it is another facet of superstition to expect the astrologer to be clairvoyant and reel off an inventory of personal trivia. If this is what you want, then you are really not going to get the best of what astrology has to offer.

The reason astrologers ask questions is, usually, because they do not want to waste time guessing those superficial facts, which are already perfectly obvious to you. They wish instead to spend that time getting to the root of your problems. Accordingly, the questions will usually concern your early life and environment to discover your subjective view of your life.

You could think of the horoscope as a map. The extent of its information is limited to a flat, two-dimensional list of possibilities.

A map can contain a lot of information, of course. If it is of a town it can tell you the names and show the positions of the roads and main buildings. However, it cannot show what condition they are in.

It can also tell you the population figure. But the character of the people cannot be deduced from such a number any more than can the type of materials they use to build their dwellings, or whether the residents like, love, or even respect their environment.

It is much the same with a horoscope. A telling profile can be constructed from the bare bones of a chart without your help. However, this can be only two-dimensional until the astrologer has interacted with you on a personal level. This is the only way he or she can accurately flesh out the skeleton and, most importantly, find the life in it. Only then can the linear string of information in the chart become a living, growing, three-dimensional being.

So, please don't respond automatically to an astrologer's questions with the perennial: '. . . *You're* supposed to be telling *me* that . . .'

The view of an astrologer as a demi-god or clairvoyant can mean that his or her word is sacrosanct. But there is another extreme that results from this view. Where a too-believing attitude may eagerly excuse or overlook error, the sceptic, who is also superstitious underneath, will not permit such an infirmity and will jump on an error with glee.

There are hundreds of elements in a horoscope, which can combine to produce a vast repertoire of possible characteristics. Modern astrologers have an additional complication which arises from their efforts to focus on the deeper psychological aspects of human nature. In order to ensure that you get an accurate and unbiased interpretation of your horoscope, they must try to empty themselves mentally and emotionally before each consultation. They must forget not only themselves — their personal needs, likes, dislikes and prejudices — but also any previous client's life, personality and problems.

To be fair to the honest astrologers, it would be as unreasonable to expect them to hit precisely upon every detail of your character and life as it would to expect every doctor to know all the symptoms of, and cures for, every illness. We allow that doctors may need to refer patients to other doctors and, if necessary, go through months of tests to enable them to arrive at a correct diagnosis, remedy and prognosis for a single illness. But because of their status, astrologers are apparently expected to bring someone's whole life and nature together in a coherent and accurate summary in one sitting.

Obviously, this is just not possible. And it means that the astrologer will very likely make mistakes. Aleister Crowley may have acquired a bad reputation for some of his activities, but he was accurate in his sardonic observation of astrology:

> *Astrologers sometimes make mistakes. From this fact, which even they are scarcely sufficiently brazen to dispute, it follows with mathematical certainty that astrology is not a science but a sham, a quackery and a fraud. Contrast its shameful uncertainty with medicine, where no doctor ever lost a patient; with law where no lawyer ever lost a case ...!*
>
> (THE COMPLETE ASTROLOGICAL WRITINGS,
> AS QUOTED IN A. T. MANN'S THE ROUND ART)

And, I would add, with science, where every universal law ever discovered was an absolute.

THE BALANCED WAY   If you approach your astrologer with openness, but also with discrimination, you should find that the insights you gain into your actions, motives and life, will be a *continual* source of relief and enrichment, not just a momentary one confined to the occasion of your horoscope reading.

It is true you may be expressing your greatest potential at the time of your visit to the astrologer. But our potential grows as we grow and, theoretically — barring a major physical or mental impediment — we should never reach its uppermost limits. Which means your reading should become more revealing as time passes and your life and character unfold.

Consequently, before you reject something the astrologer says about your nature because you don't immediately identify with it, consider the possibility (but naturally, don't automatically assume) that the described characteristic may not yet have surfaced. If you reject it too hastily it could mean a missed opportunity to recognise and integrate it into your life just that bit sooner, if it does exist as part of your nature.

Give the astrologer a chance — *once you are satisfied that he or she is sincere and competent* — to use his or her particular skills for your benefit, and for the astrologer's benefit too. For when you go to an astrologer, it is an exchange. It is not a lecture from a teacher to a pupil. The astrologer, whether either of you is aware of it or not, is going to learn as much from you as you are from him or her.

3 PRACTICALITIES

THE PRACTITIONERS

Here we will look at the astrologers themselves and the manner in which some of them approach their art. I have narrowed this down to types who, I feel, would fall prey to the usual pitfalls of being an astrologer. These are:

1. the over-enthusiastic beginner;
2. the experienced astrologer who is too rigidly ruled by tradition;
3. the astrologer who purposely creates an aura of mystery at the expense of his or her client;
4. the charlatan, who is in the business really only for money.

First of all I should clarify that there are beginners, traditionalists and clairvoyant types who are capable and sincere. I am not trying to denigrate those whose attitude or approach does not comply with my own standards. I am simply attempting to give the layperson a set of guidelines to enable him or her to spot those astrologers who may not be particularly discriminating in their methods, nor honest in their motives.

THE BEGINNER   It is difficult for the layperson to tell just how much experience an astrologer may have had. This is especially a problem if the astrologer is unknown to the general public and, naturally, to the client in particular. The danger here is that, as with any occupation or subject, a beginner who has some knowledge can easily appear experienced to someone who has no knowledge of the subject matter at all. Fortunately, rank beginners will largely confine themselves to practising on friends and relatives who are aware of their inexperience and will therefore be much less likely to be affected by fanciful embellishments or errors of judgment.

However, those beginners who have graduated from this harmless stage and set themselves up in practice prematurely will have more people taking notice of what they are saying. The 'rookie' astrologer is dangerous because he or she is at a point where they are more prone to misuse their untried skills. This is a delicate juncture in the career of a budding astrologer because a little knowledge and a smattering of self-confidence can be catalysed by zealous enthusiasm into gross misunderstanding and error.

THE TRADITIONALIST   These astrologers may have a thorough knowledge of astrology. They may make calculations with a speed that stuns and give the impression of confidently knowing all the answers. And so they may — at least those they have learned by rote.

Such astrologers are able to reel off a string of uncannily accurate statements. Yet they are bits of information which are often totally unrelated; often random observations. If you are at all impressionable or in a state of indecision you may believe all of them, when in fact they may not all necessarily be true. They may even result in considerable anxiety, or tragedy. Stay away from this type of astrologer.

THE MYSTIC   Then there are astrologers who have convinced themselves they are also clairvoyants. Although there is nothing wrong with clairvoyant/astrologers, who may well have some ability with predictive astrology in particular, one should steer clear of the deluded ones. They are easy to spot: they are usually a walking occult cliché with trimmings and name to match, their number one aim being *awe*, at any cost.

Discrimination is necessary, as always, to distinguish between the clairvoyant and honest astrologers who simply enjoy their trappings, and those who are interested only in the show they are exhibiting rather than in the welfare of their clients.

THE CHARLATAN   These astrologers may be one or a combination of any or all of the foregoing. They should also be easily distinguishable because they will give themselves away by displaying at least one of the previously described characteristics. They have no interest whatsoever in you or your problems, although obviously there may be a veneer of caring which should be easily detectable for what it is. However, they will trip themselves up sooner or later, so the danger from this type is probably minimal.

Which category an inferior astrologer falls into is not really the issue in the end. It is just a convenient way of describing their trademarks more clearly. Underneath all of these are plain incompetence or insincerity, born out of either a lack of awareness or caring for anyone but themselves.

In all cases, random predictions that are unrelated to anything may be made in a way that defies contradiction or modification: You are going to have an accident ... lose your job ... part with your husband/wife ...!' Or there will be an overstressing of 'evil' portents: 'There is an *evil* aspect between the *malefic* planets which will cause you *terrible troubles*!' So that you can almost hear the swish of a cloak and the bubbling of a cauldron.

Or you might get a long list of instructions, which sound more like orders: 'You *must* not go against this influence ... you *must* not go overseas now!' ... all geared at the raising of your eyebrows at your astrologer's amazing canniness and power.

It should be clear by now that there are more dangers inherent in the apparently simple task of finding an astrologer than the reader may previously have imagined. To impress this upon you, I have again resorted to the use of extreme examples. And I have caused them to be guilty of the worst offences possible to drive the point home and give a feeling for what is behind any mask that may be presented.

Now to backpedal a little to bring the matter back into perspective.

Despite the necessity for caution, there are in fact relatively inexperienced astrologers who, through not being too set in the ways of tradition, are plastic and open enough to have remarkable insight. Similarly, there are astrologers of long experience who have the seasoned courage to step confidently into people's lives and capably help them grapple with their most devastating problems.

Even those astrologers who make predictions on a grandiose scale are not necessarily driven solely by sensationalism or even by the desire for power. Sometimes there is no more than a desire for some recognition of their dedication to a type of work that so many unhesitatingly demean and ridicule without honestly giving it a fair go. Most human beings need some degree of respect and appreciation. Few would be prepared to press on wholly unaffected by the scorn with which many astrologers are treated. Many of them resort to the prediction of catastrophes, or other worldwide awakeners, as a desperate means to redeem their self-respect. Being right — and in such a major way — proves the validity of the path they have chosen to follow, which in turn proves their worth, not only to the world but also to themselves.

THE WRITTEN ANALYSIS

Many astrologers, either because of distance or because they prefer it, correspond and send written delineations and prognostications to their clients. There are certain risks to be aware of in such instances. For example, you may receive for your hard-earned dollar a duplicated set of sheets, or computerised printout, listing your characteristics like a stock inventory.

No one is a list of unrelated characteristics, and this sort of partial and casual reading is little more than a glorified extension of Sun-sign delineation. Admittedly, it can be informative. However, usually no effort is made to integrate all the diverse factors into the unique whole that is the individual. Horoscope integration is by far the most difficult, and time-consuming, part of horoscope interpretation. And it is also the most important part.

If you know that this is what you are going to receive, and you are satisfied with this, that is fine — although this type of reading can be misleading. However, if this is, in fact, all you want, I suggest you pay the few dollars it costs to have your chart erected (as offered by many computer companies, for example) so that you know which signs and houses your planets are in, and then buy a reputable book that contains the meanings of these positions and the various aspects between the planets.

There are vast quantities of easy-to-understand astrology books on the market which contain this information. If you team up with a few similarly interested friends it will cost you less as you can share the purchased book between you.

Those who want more than this should clarify their requirements with their prospective astrologer *before* they send off any money. Some astrologers send questionnaires in answer to enquiries, which state more or less what to expect. Generally, it is a good idea to establish beforehand what the astrologer specialises in, if anything, or whether he or she covers a range of areas.

For example, one person might want to know about financial investment while another wants a more psychological or esoteric interpretation.

THE FEE

And finally — the fee. There are astrologers who charge little and give much. And there are those who charge much yet give little that is of any worth. There are also those whose fees are high, yet who give every penny's worth, and sometimes more. And there are those who modify their rates according to the income of the client.

In the end, however, one cannot put a price tag on astrology. Its value is wholly relative to the individual.

4 CONCLUSION

In the words of the great astrologer and philosopher, Dane Rudhyar (1895–1986):

> *No birth-chart is better than any other. One is always better for some one purpose. But as all purposes are equally valuable and necessary in the economy of the greater whole, each man's chart is better for the purposes of his life than is anybody else's.*

THE ASTROLOGY OF PERSONALITY

APPENDIX —
ASCENDANT SIGNS

If you want to get a rough idea of your Ascendant, or Rising Sign, check the following table. (Remember, this is only very approximate because Rising Signs vary according to the latitude of the birthplace. These signs will be exactly as listed only on or near to the equator. Check the preceding signs, if you were born closer to the earlier hour listed, or following signs, if you were born nearer to the later hour, should you be in any doubt.) You will probably be able to work out which is most relevant from the descriptions. However, owing to the fact that there are, as already mentioned, 10 separate bodies (planets, including the Sun and Moon) which can fall in, and therefore emphasise, any of the signs of the zodiac, for greatest accuracy, you should contact an astrologer or an astrological computing service. (You can find them in local astrology magazines or journals.)

SUN SIGN

TIME OF BIRTH

	ARIES	TAURUS	GEMINI	CANCER	LEO
6 – 8 am	ARIES	TAURUS	CANCER	LEO	VIRGO
8 – 10 am	TAURUS	GEMINI	LEO	VIRGO	LIBRA
10 – 12 pm	GEMINI	CANCER	VIRGO	LIBRA	SCORPIO
12 – 2 pm	CANCER	LEO	LIBRA	SCORPIO	SAGITT.
2 – 4 pm	LEO	VIRGO	SCORPIO	SAGITT.	CAPRIC.
4 – 6 pm	VIRGO	LIBRA	SAGITT.	CAPRIC.	AQUAR.
6 – 8 pm	LIBRA	SCORPIO	CAPRIC.	AQUAR.	PISCES
8 – 10 pm	SCORPIO	SAGITT.	AQUAR.	PISCES	ARIES
10 – 12 am	SAGITT.	CAPRIC.	PISCES	ARIES	TAURUS
12 – 2 am	CAPRIC.	AQUAR.	ARIES	TAURUS	GEMINI
2 – 4 am	AQUAR.	PISCES	TAURUS	GEMINI	CANCER
4 – 6 am	PISCES	ARIES	GEMINI	CANCER	LEO

♍ VIRGO	♎ LIBRA	♏ SCORPIO	♐ SAGITT.	♑ CAPRIC.	♒ AQUAR.	♓ PISCES
LIBRA	SCORPIO	SAGITT.	CAPRIC.	AQUAR.	PISCES	ARIES
SCORPIO	SAGITT.	CAPRIC.	AQUAR.	PISCES	ARIES	TAURUS
SAGITT.	CAPRIC.	AQUAR.	PISCES	ARIES	TAURUS	SAGITT.
CAPRIC.	AQUAR.	PISCES	ARIES	TAURUS	GEMINI	CAPRIC.
AQUAR.	PISCES	ARIES	TAURUS	GEMINI	CANCER	AQUAR.
PISCES	ARIES	TAURUS	GEMINI	CANCER	LEO	PISCES
ARIES	TAURUS	GEMINI	CANCER	LEO	VIRGO	ARIES
TAURUS	GEMINI	CANCER	LEO	VIRGO	LIBRA	TAURUS
GEMINI	CANCER	LEO	VIRGO	LIBRA	SCORPIO	SAGITT.
CANCER	LEO	VIRGO	LIBRA	SCORPIO	SAGITT.	CAPRIC.
LEO	VIRGO	LIBRA	SCORPIO	SAGITT.	CAPRIC.	AQUAR.
VIRGO	LIBRA	SCORPIO	SAGITT.	CAPRIC.	AQUAR.	PISCES

REFERENCES

Allen, Richard Hinckley. *Star Names: Their Lore and Meaning*. Dover Publications, Inc., New York, 1963.

Arroyo, Stephen. *Astrology, Karma and Transformation: The Inner Dimensions of the Birth Chart*. CRCS, Washington, 1978.

Barnhart, Clarence L., and Robert, K., (eds). *The World Book Dictionary*. Doubleday, Chicago, 1979.

Bessy, Maurice. *A Pictorial History of Magic and the Supernatural*. Spring Books (Hamlyn), Middlesex, 1964.

Bloch, Marc Leopold. *The Historian's Craft*. Manchester University Press, Manchester, 1954.

Bohannan, Paul. 'Time, Rhythm, and Pace', *Science* 80. American Association for the Advancement of Science, Washington, March/April 1980.

Campbell, Joseph. *The Way of the Animal Powers: Historical Atlas of World Mythology*, vol. 1. Times Books, London, 1984.

Capra, Fritjof. *The Tao of Physics*. Fontana, London, 1976.

Cornell, Howard Leslie. *Encyclopaedia of Medical Astrology*. Samuel Weiser Inc., New York, and Llewellyn Publications, St Paul, 1972.

Costigan, Kelly. 'Cabin Fever', *Forbes*, 20 May. Forbes Inc., New York, 20 May 1985.

Duncan, A. M. *Copernicus*. David and Charles, U.K., 1976.

Gauquelin, Michel. *Astrology and Science*. Peter Davies, London, 1970.

Greene, Liz. *The Astrology of Fate*. George Allen and Unwin, London, 1984.

———. *Relating: An Astrological Guide to Living with Others*. Samuel Weiser, New York, 1978.

———. *Saturn: A New Look at an Old Devil*. Samuel Weiser, New York, 1976.

Gribbin, John. 'Precise Measurements of Nothing Pin Down the Universe', *New Scientist*. New Science Publications, London, 15 December, 1983.

Grimal, Pierre (ed.). *Larousse World Mythology*. Hamlyn, Middlesex, 1973.

Grinnell, Dhruva. 'Three Structural Metaphors for the Signs of the Zodiac', *Australian Astrologers Journal*. Australian Astrological Cooperative (Vic.), Autumn 1980.

Gwynne, Peter. 'They're Close to Deciding the Fate of the Universe, *Popular Science*. Times Mirror Magazines, Inc., New York, December 1980.

Hales, Dianne. 'The Times of Your Life', *Next*. Litton Magazines, New York, July/August 1980.

Hand, Robert. *Planets in Composite: Analyzing Human Relationships*. Para Research, Massachusetts, 1975.

Hesiod, (tr. Dorothea Wender). *Hesiod and Theognis*. Penguin, Middlesex, 1973.

Hewitt, Paul G. *Conceptual Physics: A New Introduction to Your Environment*. Little, Brown and Co., Boston, 1974.

Hilts, Len. 'Clocks That Make Us Run', *Omni*. New York, September 1984.

Hoyle, Fred. *Nicolaus Copernicus*. Heinemann, London, 1973.

I Ching or Book of Changes, The (trs Richard Wilhelm; Cary F. Baynes). Bollingen Series XIX, Princeton University Press, New Jersey, 1967.

Jansky, Robert Carl. *Astrology, Nutrition and Health*. Para Research, Massachusetts, 1977.

Jekyll, Gertrude. *The Gardener's Essential*. Breslich and Foss, London, 1983.

Judson, Horace Freeland. *The Search for Solutions*. Hutchinson, London, 1980.

Jung, Carl G., (tr. R. F. C. Hull). *The Undiscovered Self*. Routledge and Kegan Paul, London, 1974.

———, (tr. R. F. C. Hull). *Synchronicity: An Acausal Connecting Principle*. Princeton University Press, 1973.

———, (tr. R. F. C. Hull). *The Collected Works*, vol. 8: 'The Structure and Dynamics of the Psyche'. Routledge and Kegan Paul, London, 1969.

————, (tr. R. F. C. Hull). *The Collected Works*, vol. 9, part II, 'Aion': 'Researches into the Phenomenology of the Self'. Routledge and Kegan Paul, London, 1968.

Jurtman, Richard J. 'The Effects of Light on the Human Body', *Scientific American*. New York, July 1975.

Kahler, Erich. *The Meaning of History*. Chapman and Hall, London, 1964.

Kenton, Warren. *Astrology: The Celestial Mirror*. Thames and Hudson, London, 1974.

Lilly, William. 'Epistle to the Student of Astrology', *An Introduction to Astrology*. George Bell and Sons, London, 1878.

Lindsay, Jack. *Origins of Astrology*. Frederick Muller, London, 1971.

McIntosh, Christopher. *The Astrologers and Their Creed*. Arrow, London, 1971.

McLeish, Kenneth. *Children of the Gods: The Complete Myths and Legends of Ancient Greece*. Longman Group Ltd, Essex, 1983.

Mann, A.T. *The Round Art: The Astrology of Time and Space*. Paper Tiger, Dragonsworld, Surrey, 1979.

Martin, Charles-Noël, (tr. B. B. Rafter). *The Thirteen Steps to the Atom: A Photographic Exploration*. Harrap, London, 1959.

Moore, Patrick. *New Concise Atlas of the Universe*. Mitchell Beazley, London, 1978.

———— and Hardy, David. *The New Challenge of the Stars*. Hutchinson, Melbourne, 1977.

Murchie, Guy. *Music of the Spheres*, vol. 1. Dover, New York, 1967.

Naylor, P. I. H. *Astrology: A Fascinating History*. Wilshire, California, 1972.

Pagan, Isobelle M. *From Pioneer to Poet*. Theosophical Publishing House, London, 1969.

Papon, Donald (Zolar). *The Lure of the Heavens: A History of Astrology*. Samuel Weiser, New York, 1980.

Playfair, Guy Lyon, and Hill, Scott. *The Cycles of Heaven*. Pan, London, 1979.

Plinius Secundus, Gaius, (tr. H. Rackham). *Natural History*, vol. 1. Loeb Classical Library, Heinemann, London, 1938–63.

Reagan, David. 'Electrical Responses Evoked from the Human Brain', *Scientific American*. New York, December 1979.

Ronan, Colin A. *Changing Views of the Universe*. Eyre and Spottiswoode, London, 1961.

Rudhyar, Dane. *Astrological Insights into the Spiritual Life*. ASI Publishers Inc. New York, 1979.

———. *Astrology and the Modern Psyche*. CRCS, Washington, 1976.

———. *The Astrology of Personality*. Doubleday, New York, 1970.

———. *The Pulse of Life: New Dynamics in Astrology*. Shambala Publications Inc., California, 1970.

Secret of the Golden Flower, The: A Chinese Book of Life, (trs Richard Wilhelm; Cary F. Baynes. Routledge and Kegan Paul, London, 1962.

Shil-Ponde. *Hindu Astrology (Joytisha-Shastra)*. Sagar, New Delhi, 1975.

Thompson, Marcia J. and Harsha, David W. 'Our Rhythms Still Follow the African Sun', *Psychology Today*. Ziff-Davis, New York, January 1984.

Tyl, Noel Jan. *Holistic Astrology: The Analysis of Inner and Outer Environments*. Llewellyn Publications, St Paul, 1980.

Walker, D. P. *Spiritual and Demonic Magic from Ficino to Campanella*. The Warburg Institute, University of London, London, 1958.

Wilson, John M. (ed.). *The Farmer's Dictionary*, vol. I. A. Fullerton & Co., Edinburgh, no date.

Yellow Emperor's Classic of Internal Medicine, The, (tr. Ilza Veith). University of California Press, California, 1966.

Zukav, Gary. *The Dancing Wu Li Masters*. Fontana, London, 1980.

RECOMMENDED READING

Avery, Jeanne. *The Rising Sun: Your Astrological Mask*. Doubleday, New York, 1982.

Edmonds, Dodie and Allan. *Child Signs: Understanding Your Child Through Astrology*. CRCS Publications, New York, 1978.

Green, Liz. *Saturn: A New Look at an Old Devil*. Samuel Weiser Inc., New York, 1976.

———. *The Astrology of Fate*. George Allen & Unwin Ltd, London, 1984.

———. *Relating: An Astrological Guide to Living with Others on a Small Planet*. Coventure Ltd, London, 1978.

Johfra Astrology, (tr. Jan Michael). V.O.C. Angel Books, Amsterdam, 1981.

March, Marion D., and McEvers, Joan. *The Only Way to Learn Astrology*, vol. 1, 'Basic Principles'. ACS Publications, 1981.

Moore, Marcia, and Douglas, Mark. *Astrology*. Arcane Publications, Maine, 1971.

Pagan, Isabelle M. *From Pioneer to Poet*. Theosophical Publishing House London Ltd, London, 1969.

Sakoian, Frances, and Acker, Louis S. *The Astrologer's Handbook*. Harper & Row, New York, 1973.

Sasportas, Howard. *The Twelve Houses: An Introduction to the Houses in Astrological Interpretation*. The Aquarian Press, Northamptonshire, 1985.

To find computer company listings to obtain birth data only (specify that you want the information written in English — sometimes it is printed out in astrological symbology): consult local astrology magazines such as (in Australia) the *Astrological Monthly Review*, edited by Ray Webb; or (Australia and overseas) *Horoscope*, edited in the USA by Julia A. Wagner; or contact any astrological association which will be listed in the phone book.